COOL CAREERS WITHOUT COLLEGE FOR

PEOPLE WHO LOVE TO ORGANIZE, MANAGE, AND PLAN

COOL CAREERS WITHOUT COLLEGE FOR PEOPLE WHO LOVE TO ORGANIZE, MANAGE, AND PLAN

ROBERT GREENBERGER

The Rosen Publishing Group, Inc., New York

Published in 2007 by The Rosen Publishing Group, Inc.
29 East 21st Street, New York, NY 10010

Library of Congress Cataloging-in-Publication Data

Greenberger, Robert.
Cool careers without college for people who love to organize, manage, and plan/Robert Greenberger.—1st ed.
     p. cm.—(Cool careers without college)
Includes index.
ISBN 1-4042-0752-X (library binding)
1. Home economics—Vocational guidance. I. Title. II. Series.
TX147.G72 2007
640.23—dc22
                                                              2005031276

Manufactured in the United States of America

CONTENTS

Introduction 7

1 Personal Assistant 9

2 Fund-Raiser 20

3 Retail Manager 31

4 Wedding/Party
Planner 42

5 Event Coordinator 52

6 Trade-Show Organizer 63

7 Professional Organizer 76

8 Life Coach 86

9 Operations Manager 94

10 Merchandise Planner/
Assistant Planner 102

11 Travel Coordinator 111

12 Auctioneer 120

13 Import/Export
Specialist 131

Glossary 139

Index 141

INTRODUCTION

Some people will look at a task and immediately feel overwhelmed. At the same time, others can look at the same task and instantly recognize what needs to be done and how best to accomplish the goal. Even though it's the same task, people approach it with different attitudes and ideas.

For those people who work well under pressure, there are numerous challenging and creative fields where their skills can be used without benefit of a college degree. Organizing certainly means more than determining the best way to stack boxes or arrange a closet. Instead, in many cases it can mean sorting out the details of someone else's life and making things easier and more efficient.

For those who like to work with other people, there are many options available for a person who is naturally organized and on the ball. This is also usually a person who appreciates a good puzzle or enjoys solving problems on his or her own. Being an independent thinker can bring tremendous satisfaction and rewards.

In the following chapters, you will be given a brief introduction to many fields where an organized person could flourish in the current and future job market. Organizing offers tremendous opportunities for helping others in the short term as well as the future. As a natural organizer you may help create memories that will bring others satisfaction or you might help generate money that can help those who are less fortunate. All in all, applying your abilities will bring countless personal rewards.

1

PERSONAL ASSISTANT

Since the Industrial Revolution introduced the concept of the modern office,
there has been a need for clerks,
secretaries, and administrative
assistants. According to the
United States Department of
Labor, there were 1.4 million
office administrators in 2000.
Careers as personal assistants
are far-reaching, with positions

in many areas ranging from home health care to running what is essentially a small business.

Description

The personal assistant is responsible for organizing someone else's life, running errands, and making sure things large and small are accomplished in a timely fashion. Personal assistants have to remember many details, from a boss's spouse's birthday to picking up the dry cleaning. In some cases, the personal assistant for a corporate officer will be expected to blur the line between professional obligations and personal ones. In just about every case, the hours for personal assistants are long.

Depending upon the position, the personal assistant will be required to know basic computer software such as Microsoft Word, Excel, and Outlook. In these days of wireless technology, you are also likely to encounter a variety of hand-held devices, too, such as cell phones and PDAs (personal digital assistants). For those caring for the ill, understanding IVs, catheters, pill schedules, and oxygen tanks is required.

Of the jobs posted, the most glamorous might sound like the following: "A-List Celebrity/Actor seeks personal assistant. Live-out position with travel. Will support with all aspects of her personal life. Arrange family, personal, and business matters. Plan events for business and pleasure.

Assist in maintaining households. Requires a flexible schedule for travel. Quick thinking, resourceful, and being able to switch gears is necessary."

Sounds exciting, right? But look more closely at the description. You will also be asked to do mundane household tasks as part of the job. Maintaining the house could mean time spent food shopping or even dusting. This description sounds a little less thrilling, right?

To qualify, the ad also states: "Three years minimum serving as a personal assistant or equivalent experience, excellent com-

Keeping track of appointments for a celebrity, media personality, or executive can be a daunting task, especially since changes are common and have the potential of shifting his or her entire schedule. In many cases, personal assistants must also be familiar with a wide variety of electronic gadgets to manage schedule changes while in transit.

munication skills, must have prior entertainment/production experience."

In the Princeton Review's *Best Entry-Level Jobs*, one personal assistant to a celebrity said, "I was too naïve at that point to know [that I should negotiate my starting salary]. It could've been negotiable, but it was so exciting to be offered the job that I didn't ask." Asked to name the fringe benefits of their job, assistants list "free travel and life experience" and "the opportunity to know an American legend on a personal basis." For a personal assistant to a major fashion designer, the major perk was "the clothes, hands down. We had the best wardrobes in town..."

Positions available as personal assistants for celebrities are infrequent opportunities. Many more PA jobs come from the corporate world. A different ad for a major clothing chain was looking for an executive administrative assistant who would be required to do the following:

- Manage executive calendar and schedule appointments
- Screen incoming calls and correspondence and respond independently when possible
- Arrange programs, events, or conferences by reserving facilities and issuing information or invitations
- Direct preparation of records such as agenda, notices, minutes, and resolutions for departmental meetings
- Type correspondence including letters, memos, forms, etc.
- Arrange complex and detailed travel plans and itineraries and compile documents for traveling
- Assist with preparation of departmental reports
- Coordinate recruitment process with HR and colleges for hiring assistant buyers

- Edit and process departmental timesheets for payroll purposes
- Order and keep inventory of supplies
- Coordinate all record keeping as required

It sounds like the description of a secretary; well, maybe more than a typical secretary, hence the word "executive" in the title. These days, calling someone a secretary might seem a little outdated, so the title has morphed into administrative assistant, personal assistant, and beyond. The duties, though, have not necessarily changed.

The requirements in this case include: "...a seasoned administrative professional with at least three years of office management experience. Excellent verbal and written communication skills are paramount, as are solid organizational and multitasking skills. Computer proficiency in MS Office is an absolute must. This person must also be flexible to work overtime as needed and capable of handling time-sensitive and confidential information."

Why do executives, professionals, or even actors need a personal assistant? *Realtor* magazine says, "Hiring a personal assistant can boost your production from mid-level performance to top-producing status. But your level of success depends on what you want the assistant to do—secretarial work or hands-on real estate support—whether the person is licensed or unlicensed, what you'll pay, and how well you

Actress Jennifer Aniston *(left)*, who played the character Rachel Green in the NBC situation comedy *Friends,* is seen in this scene with actor Eddie Cahill, who was cast as her personal assistant. Seeing personal assistants on television and in films has possibly increased the demand for these positions.

prepare the person for the job." Many of those qualities will apply to other fields as well.

On Australia's Girl.com (www.girl.com.au/pa_office manager.htm), an interview with a typical executive personal assistant, a twenty-nine-year-old woman named Fiona Wilson, was posted. "I am the personal assistant to the three directors of a multimedia company. My role can consist of anything from taking minutes to organizing functions or programming a Web site.

"Working as a personal assistant can be a great step to running your own business or working out which field you want to work in without having the qualifications in that field. In my case, my previous PA role was for a small business and I learnt the whole business back to front. Essentially I can apply that to any role I want or establish my own business. In this role now I have learnt how bigger corporations work and the importance of procedures and foundations for setting up a successful company.

"I love the challenge of the day. You never know what might land in my tray. For instance last week I organized a proposal for a Web site, booked training sessions for clients, held two client training sessions, wrote and sent a weekly newsletter to our members, did HTML and Lotus Notes programming to update our Web site, went to a fashion launch for a client, took minutes at four board meetings, organized a breakfast function, organized a promotion for one of our Web sites, finalized printing requirements for a client, prepared staff manuals for the new recruits, sent RSVPs for the directors to attend functions, and so on...

"The best advice I can give is great communication and time management are the foundations for anywhere you want to go. Understanding how everything works makes you a good boss for the future."

Education and Training

Personal assistants like being in control. A good personal assistant has a take-charge personality, likes to keep things moving, and can usually see what's coming up a day, a week, or a month down the road. To prepare for a job as a personal assistant, high school students are encouraged to take English, speech, communications, math, sociology, history, typing, bookkeeping, and computer classes. Above all, you need to be organized. Having experience with computers, various types of software (both PC and Macintosh), knowledge of MS Office, and a good handle on time management is essential. You also need basic secretarial skills and a lot of creativity (especially when you are assisting multiple people who all want things done as a priority). Statistics show that time spent successfully managing extracurricular activities such as athletic teams, scouting troops, and community fund-raisers can help young people develop the types of skills they will one day need as personal or executive assistants.

Salary

The 2002 median salary for administrative assistants/secretaries in the United States was $33,400. In corporations it ran higher, at $36,800, while local government workers earned $34,600, and state employees earned $31,200. With 4.1 million secretaries in 2002, the position is seen as one that will not vanish anytime soon and one that is an excellent place to begin a career.

Outlook

Working as a personal assistant is a job that has seen much growth over the past decade. And with the growing complexities of everyday life, more and more people with means have come to rely upon organized individuals to help them plan their professional and personal lives.

The book *Beyond the Red Carpet: Keys to Becoming a Successful Personal Assistant* by Dionne M. Muhammad asserts, "These machines of modern business are a

In this photograph taken in Manhattan in 2003, popular singer Mary J. Blige is helped on with a pair of shoes by a personal assistant before going on stage during her performance in the Toyota Concert Series on the NBC *Today Show* in Rockefeller Plaza.

hybrid of secretary, project manager, and confidante to their employer. Personal assistants are demanding more responsibility, autonomy, and recognition." And in her view, they're getting it.

In a *Los Angeles Times* article, one celebrity assistant's job was assessed as follows: "No longer are personal assistants simply gofers, those harried folks who appear just outside the paparazzo's frame, usually bedraggled and weighed down by luggage. They have begun to organize. They have formed associations in New York and Los Angeles. They have written how-to books and established training programs, even internships.

"In the past, people became personal assistants right out of college, for lack of a better option or because their job in show business eventually led them to one needy celebrity. Today young people are lining up to apply for the jobs that they have seen in action on any number of unscripted TV shows." To be sure, being a personal assistant can be both interesting and rewarding.

FOR MORE INFORMATION

ORGANIZATIONS
American Management Association
1601 Broadway
New York, NY 10019
(212) 586-8100
Web site: http://www.amanet.org/index.htm

National Association of Executive Secretaries and Administrative Assistants
900 S. Washington Street, Suite G-13

Falls Church, VA 22046
(703) 237-8616
Web site: http://www.naesaa.com

National Management Association
2210 Arbor Boulevard
Dayton, OH 45439
(937) 294-0421
Web site: http://www.nma1.org

WEB SITES

Fab Job.com
http://www.fabjob.com/celebrity.asp
This Web site includes an informative article about working as a celebrity assistant.

Fashion Job Review.com
http://www.fashionjobreview.com/Celebrity_Personal_Assistant.html
A Web site that provides a nice overview of a celebrity assistant's tasks.

BOOKS

Beckel, Heather. *Be a Kickass Assistant: How to Get from a Grunt Job to a Great Career*. New York, NY: Warner Business Books, 2002.
Duncan, Melba J. *The New Executive Assistant: Advice for Succeeding in Your Career*. New York, NY: McGraw-Hill, 1997.
Longson, Sally. *Getting a Top Job as a Personal Assistant*. London, England: Kogan Page, 2002.
Muhammad, Dionne M. *Beyond the Red Carpet: Keys to Becoming a Successful Personal Assistant*. New York, NY: Authorhouse, 2004.

2

FUND-RAISER

Everyone needs money. In addition to the money that people need to survive, some people and organizations need donations from the public and private sectors. This money usually helps finance medical research, sponsors fund-raising activities for special causes, or even helps politicians run for elected office. In just about every case, fund-raisers are needed to champion these needs and causes.

Description

Fund-raisers work for charities, belong to corporations, or are members of groups that are hired for special occasions. Fund-raising—an outgrowth of old-fashioned philanthropy—is considered one of the ten largest industries in the United States, according to the *Encyclopedia of Careers and Vocational Guidance*. During 2000, more than $200 billion was raised through charitable giving by public and private donors.

The people who do this work are described on the University of Virginia Web site as "'fund-raising' or 'development,' professionals who research, plan, and carry out strategies to convince individuals, companies, foundations, and governments to donate money to their organizations." Their work varies, depending on the size the organization. The larger the organization is, the larger its development staff. In cases such as this, each person working on the development staff will have a small function. For instance, an urban hospital usually has a large development staff, while a small nonprofit organization often has a single executive director who oversees the entire fund-raising operation.

Fund-raisers usually focus on one project at a time such as raising money to build a new church or financing the annual running of the Special Olympics. Larger organizations,

United Way campaign chairman A. Dale Cannady announces the total monies raised during a 2001 annual fund-raising event at the Richmond Center in Richmond, Virginia. Fund-raising can be an extremely fulfilling career, especially if you can make a positive impact on the lives of those people who are disadvantaged or in need of financial help for long-term medical expenses.

such as the American Heart Association, have fund-raising events throughout the year, but the organizers usually run only one campaign at a time. Fund-raising can be done to raise money for education, the environment, health services, the arts, or charities.

A fund-raiser working for a firm will be asked to help with a campaign. The person will meet with the organization to find out the goal of the event, the timetable, and the method desired. Research will then be required to examine the reality of the goal, comparing it with the organization's previous efforts, studying the target group of donors, and determining how the event will be publicized. Then the fund-raiser will study who else will be seeking funds in the same area at the same time. Once compiled, the results are used to create a feasibility study, and from there, a final game plan.

The work itself can vary. Fund-raisers organize a variety of activities that may include raffles, carnivals, phone campaigns, dinners, athletic events, mailings, and even performances. Each of these has to be tailored in some way to the organization and its goal, then planned, advertised, and executed. As a result, the job can be hectic.

Specific tasks include:

- Creating budgets, tracking income and expenses, and recording and processing donations
- Writing grant proposals and tracking their progress
- Planning and participating in fund-raising events
- Training and directing volunteers and staff
- Writing publicity materials such as press releases and brochures
- Researching potential donors and developing relationships with them
- Attending public events to promote the agency
- Preparing reports and analysis of fund-raising trends and activities

Other times, fund-raisers turn to more sedate approaches to reach their objective. One example of this approach would be setting up a series of talks to focus attention on the problem the money would help address. In some instances, such as in situations that focus on rare diseases or social problems, the public needs to be educated before they are asked for donations.

This is closer to the description of a developer, someone who will develop larger bequests of money, either from philanthropic organizations or wealthy individuals. From there, matching funds from smaller organizations or individuals may be sought.

At Getthatgig.com, a Web site for young people that lists internship and entry-level job opportunities, there is a profile of Stephanie Cesna, who was the manager/volunteer coordinator for the 2004 America's Walk for Diabetes in Chicago. She spent a year planning the event, which required her to coordinate all the volunteers and set up registration booths, food tents, sponsor tents, and rest stops during the walk. There were more than 100 volunteers and more than 1,000 participants in the walk. Cesna's goal was to raise $350,000, a number that she met.

"Fund-raising is a very results-driven field," Cesna says. "People who hire fund-raisers want to see that a person is motivated, energetic, and able to prove that they can meet, if not surpass, goals. Often you start at the bottom—possibly as

Citizens in Boise, Idaho, are seen in this photograph writing personal checks to assist in the relief efforts after the tragic South Asian tsunami of 2004. Dunya Wojcik, one of the event's organizers, donated all of the proceeds from the event to relief organizations, including Doctors Without Borders, and Oxfam's Asia Earthquake Fund.

an assistant. This may not sound too exciting, but the learning curve is amazingly fast and the potential to absorb fund-raising tips is incredible. At my previous job, I was initially just a volunteer coordinator. But I took an interest in the goals of the organization and made an effort to cooperate and assist the director of development. Eventually I was trained and promoted to director of public relations and volunteer development, and invited to participate in fund-raising meetings and task forces. It was a springboard into this job."

Education and Training

In order to be successful in this field, you need to know money-management skills, accounting skills, public relations savvy, marketing techniques, and how to work and communicate with people. Recommended high school courses include English, creative writing, speech, math, business, history, foreign language, bookkeeping, and computers. Personal skills needed include leadership and enthusiasm, since you're trying to convince people to contribute money to your cause.

You also need to be adaptable since quite often you will be working at the organization's headquarters, which may be cramped or less than ideal. The facilities may be temporary and the hours will certainly be irregular based on the project. A great deal of flexibility is required for anyone working as a fund-raiser. This is perhaps even more accurate for political fund-raisers than someone working for a community since candidates cover a district, state, or even the country.

Once you choose to enter this field, it is recommended that you become certified. Certificates are offered by Certified Fund Raising Executive International and need to be renewed every three years.

Salary

A starting fund-raiser can expect to earn between $20,000 and $25,000 a year. The University of Virginia Web site

How to Land a Job as a Fund-Raiser

EHow.com, a Web site of instructional information, offers the following job search tips:

- Search for Web sites of fund-raising associations and contact the companies for employment information. Be certain to speak with people who are actively involved in fund-raising. Come prepared with questions about their operation and how you might grow within the firm.
- Consult with fund-raisers at large and small fund-raising firms in your area. Ask about the pros and cons of their jobs and for ways to advance in the field.
- Understand that your first few years with a fund-raising organization will be an intensive training period, despite your college degree. You will not be involved in making decisions about any fund-raising drives. Expect your salary to reflect this.
- Receive a professional certification in fund-raising after you have made career advancements. You will raise your status and, possibly, your salary.
- Gain experience by volunteering at local events put on by schools, hospitals, churches, or political parties.

estimates that "salaries for development professionals can range from $30,000 to $150,000. Although professionals generally start out with modest salaries, successful fund-raisers can command significantly higher salaries within just a few years. Even people with only two or three years of experience are likely to earn salaries of $35,000–$40,000. With five or more years of experience, professionals can earn between $45,000 and $80,000. And senior development executives make salaries of between $75,000 to $140,000."

Outlook

Careers in fund-raising are expected to remain robust in the years ahead. Finding the work is not especially difficult. Mark J. Drozdowski writes in *The Chronicle of Higher Education*, "Take time to lurk in development-related chat rooms or bulletin-board sites and you'll find numerous examples of professionals seeking to move from the corporate world to educational fund-raising. Many of them are burned out or dissatisfied with their current lot. Others have lost their jobs or feel unstable in this shaky economy."

While planning a wedding or successful party may be fun and satisfying using the same skills, many draw a deeper and richer sense of satisfaction knowing their efforts have raised money for noble causes.

FOR MORE INFORMATION

ORGANIZATIONS

American Association of Fundraising Counsel
4700 West Lake Avenue
Glenview, IL 60025
(800) 462-2372
Web site: http://www.aafrc.org/

Association of Fundraising Professionals
1101 King Street, Suite 700
Alexandria, VA 22314
(703) 684-0410
Web site: http://www.afpnet.org/

Association of Fundraising Professionals (Canada)
275 Slater Street, Suite 900
Ottawa, ON K1P 5H9
Canada
(613) 236-0658
Web site: http://www.afpnet.org/about_afp/afp_canada/

Certified Fund Raising Executive International
4900 Seminary Road, Suite 520
Alexandria, VA 22311
(703) 370-5555
Web site: http://www.cfre.org/index.php/

WEB SITES

Charity People
http://www.charitypeople.com/
> This Web site includes job profiles and a job bulletin, and offers
> e-mail alerts for interested job seekers.

Idealist.org
http://www.nonprofits.org/
> This Web site contains an extensive database of Frequently Asked Questions (FAQs) about fund-raising.

Work with us.org
http://www.workwithus.org/
> This Web site is a gateway to the voluntary sector and features articles, resources, campaigning ideas, and more.

BOOKS

Cohen, Lilly, and Dennis R. Young. *Careers for Dreamers and Doers.* New York, NY: Foundation Center, 1989.
Lowell, Stephanie. *The Harvard Business School Guide to Careers in the Nonprofit Sector.* Boston, MA: Harvard Business School, 2000.

PERIODICALS

The Chronicle of Philanthropy
1255 23rd Street NW, Suite 700
Washington, DC 20037
(202) 466-1200
Web site: http://www.philanthropy.com
> This is a newspaper of the nonprofit world that features articles, career guidance, and a job board.

FundRaising Success
1500 Spring Garden Street, Suite 1200
Philadelphia, PA 19130
Web site: http://www.fundraisingsuccessmag.com
> This is a practical guide for those working for nonprofit organizations.

3

RETAIL MANAGER

You go into your favorite store to buy clothes or books and you see that everything is orderly, the staff is well groomed and polite, and the signs are clear and easy to understand. Behind it all stands a retail manager who brought countless elements together to make the store an inviting place.

Sales manager Irina Krupskaya works on her delivery orders in her Lane Bryant store in Skokie, Illinois. As a manager, Krupskaya has to determine which styles sell best at her location and anticipate which styles customers will be asking for during the upcoming season.

The concept of the retail department store began in the latter half of the nineteenth century, and it wasn't until the 1930s that chains—which had a single name and uniform look to each store—began growing across the United States.

Description

Retail chains began with clothing and accessories, but they now encompass almost every type of durable good. As a result, there are several chains in every category adding up to a robust field that is expected, by the U.S. Department of Labor, to grow continuously through 2012. One area of growth, electronic commerce via the Internet, is expected to have minimal impact on traditional retail stores while providing a different area of management opportunity.

While cashiers scan merchandise, and sales clerks stock shelves and greet customers, what exactly does the manager do? Retail managers hire and train staff, supervise them during operating hours, maintain the physical facilities, manage inventories, monitor expenditures and receipts, and maintain good public relations, not only with every customer but with the neighborhood where the store is located.

A job in retail management comes with high expectations. At job opportunity Web site Monster.com, career counselor Valerie Lipow wrote, "A retail manager's goal is to maximize productivity. This is tough. Store staffs likely include inexperienced, part-time or seasonal employees. Retail hours are long. Sales targets may seem unreachable. Yet, in this setting, good retail managers thrive. They are skilled in four primary areas: managing time, recruiting and supervising staff, building skilled and motivated sales and service teams, and managing change. No manager can be effective in just one of these areas. They are interrelated and interdependent."

With the larger chains, from discount retailers like Wal-Mart to upscale department stores such as Macy's, corporate leaders dictate how stores are designed, what

Part of the job of a retail manager is to keep an eye on your competition. This manager saves steps by examining a series of competitors' weekly advertisements in his local newspapers. Managers will sometimes change decisions about running sales on items depending on what local retailers are planning.

inventory is carried or placed on sale, what promotions are offered, and even how to decorate for the holidays. Effective managers follow those guidelines to the letter and then add their own touches wherever possible, denoting items that are regional favorites, such as jerseys featuring the name of a local sports team or nearby college. Some chains are stricter than others when it comes to such embellishments, and adhering to those guidelines will either prolong or curtail a manager's career.

That said, the primary goal of any retail manager is to use all the elements of a chain's guidelines in an effort to maximize overall retail sales. There will be pressure to do better than competitive chains or regional stores within the chain.

A constant in the retail business is change. As tastes evolve or new products are introduced, stores need to be adaptable to the whims of the public. As a result, a promotion that worked one holiday may be inappropriate a year later, or a display touting a product may be ignored since people are no longer interested. The retail manager needs to be flexible enough to follow the lead of the customer. If dissatisfied, the customer will shop somewhere else and the manager will face declining sales and unhappy upper management.

For people running their own retail businesses, they can test the pulse of the public and react more quickly, tailoring displays and new product arrivals to the demands of the local population. Here, the retail manager, with a smaller staff and fewer national resources, can compete with the bigger chains by adapting more rapidly to fickle customers.

Education and Training

To work your way up to a position as a retail manager, you'll need to work long hours and show that you are responsible, diplomatic, and that you can set a good example to other employees. There are no courses in this field, but English, math, marketing, and economics classes will prove useful to high school students who wish to become retail managers.

According to the Department of Labor's *Occupational Outlook Handbook*, retail managers are provided training by most of the major chain operations. Practical experience is gained through lower-level jobs, but once someone is tapped to become a manager, there is a broader array of subjects that need to be covered. The handbook says, "Classroom training may include such topics as interviewing and

COOL CAREERS WITHOUT COLLEGE

Working Your Way Up

Allyn Gibson is a retail manager in Pennsylvania for the EB Games chain. With five years of managerial experience, he began his job as a sales clerk during the summer of 1999 and never left. He notes in an interview, "Looking back I made the right choice—I could have spent $26,000 a year attending college or earn $26,000 working in retail. I began as a part-time sales associate, moved into an assistant manager position within three months, and was promoted to store manager a few months later."

Gibson enjoys his job and stresses that experience is the key to becoming a manager. "Responsibilities vary from day to day," Gibson says. "The main duty of an EB employee is to work with customers in determining their needs and selling product[s] to them, but there are store maintenance tasks, such as taking out the garbage, stocking shelves, and cleaning windows and fixtures, that must be done every day. An employee who has demonstrated selling skills, who has shown leadership, and who has proven his or her drive to succeed stands a good chance of being promoted. Retail experience counts, as does sales performance. To be considered for a management position a person needs to demonstrate his or her ability to drive sales and put money in the cash drawer.

"Retail is very much a 'learn on the job' career," Gibson continues. "As a manager I have to examine how well my staff is selling, give them guidance to improve their selling through training and role-playing, and direct them toward completing store operational tasks—like stocking the shelves, processing shipment, and cleaning the store—in a way that balances that against the need to satisfy the customer," he says. A manager has to make the store schedule, take care of customer issues, or ship products to other stores or back to the warehouse. Management has a rhythm to it, and that is both an advantage and a disadvantage. Travel is rare, and you normally spend between forty to fifty hours a week inside the store. If you work in retail you will work weekends, typically every Saturday and one or two Sundays a month. "The upshot to working weekends is that days off from work fall in the middle of the week, when banking is done, when the post office is open, when doctors' offices are open, which means that you do not need to take time off from work to do the mundane things in life that need doing."

customer service skills, employee and inventory manage-ment, and scheduling. Management trainees may be placed in one specific department for training on the job, or they may be rotated among several departments to gather a well-rounded knowledge of the store's operation. Training programs in franchises generally are extensive, covering all functions of the operation, including promotion, marketing, management, finance, purchasing, product preparation, human resource management, and compensation."

Salary

The starting salary for smaller-store retail managers is around $17,000 while the ceiling can reach as high as $100,000 based on the store, its inventory, and its location. The 2002 median salary across all fields for retail sales managers was $29,700. For nonretail sales managers such as wholesale electronic agents, professional equipment suppliers, and insurance carriers, the median income in 2002 was $53,000.

Outlook

The vast majority of retail store managers achieve their positions after years of work in the retail business, starting as stock clerks or cashiers and rising through the ranks. According to the U.S. Department of Labor, there were 2.4 million sales worker supervisors with 43 percent employed in the retail sector in 2002, with grocery stores, department stores, motor vehicle dealerships, and clothing and accessory stores among the largest employers. Another 36 percent were self-employed business owners.

The entire nonretail area of sales management is large and encompasses much not visible to the consumer. A manager in this realm, according to the Department of Labor, is responsible for supervising and coordinating "the activities of sales workers who sell industrial products, automobiles, or services such as advertising or Internet services. They may prepare budgets, make personnel decisions, devise sales-incentive programs, assign sales territories, or approve sales contracts." Like most jobs in the retail sector, jobs in retail management are expected to grow nationally over the next decade, especially in more populated areas.

FOR MORE INFORMATION

ORGANIZATIONS

International Food Service Distributors Association
201 Park Washington Court
Falls Church, VA 22046-4521
(703) 532-9400
Web site: http://www.ifdaonline.org/

National Association of Convenience Stores
1600 Duke Street

Alexandria, VA 22314-3436
(703) 684-3600
Web site: http://www.cstorecentral.com/

National Association of Display Industries
3595 Sheridan Street, Suite 200
Hollywood, FL 33021
(954) 893-7225
Web Site: http://www.nadi-global.com

National Automobile Dealers Association
8400 Westpark Drive
McLean, VA 22102-3591
(800) 821-7000
Web site: http://www.nada.org

National Retail Federation
325 7th Street, NW, Suite 1100
Washington, DC 20004
(800) 673-4692
Web site: http://www.nrf.com

Retail Council of Canada
1255 Bay Street, Suite 800
Toronto, ON M5R 2A9
Canada
(416) 922-6678
Web site: http//www.retailcouncil.org

Retail Industry Leaders Association
1700 N. Moore Street, Suite 2250
Arlington, VA 22209
(703) 841-2300
Web site: http://www.imra.org

WEB SITES

AllRetailJobs.com

http://www.allretailjobs.com/
> This Web site boasts the largest retail job board on the Internet.

CareerHunt.net

http://careerhunt.net/
> This Web site has career information about a variety of national chain stores.

Chain Store Age: An Industry Magazine on the Web

http://www.chainstoreage.com/
> This is the Web site magazine for retail executives.

Nation Job Network

http://www.nationjob.com/retail/
> This searchable career site has general information about retail jobs.

RetailManager.net

http://www.retailmanager.net/
> You can post your résumé and search for positions in retail management on this Web site.

BOOKS

Berman, Barry, and Joel R. Evans. *Retail Management: A Strategic Approach*. New York, NY: Prentice Hall, 2003.

Friedman, Harry J. *No Thanks, I'm Just Looking: Professional Retail Sales Techniques for Turning Shoppers into Buyers*. Des Moines, IA: Kendall/Hunt Publishing, 1992.

Levy, Michael, and Barton A. Weitz. *Retailing Management w/ Student Tutorial CD-ROM*, 5th ed. New York, NY: McGraw-Hill/Irwin, 2003.

Underhill, Paco. *Why We Buy: The Science of Shopping*. New York, NY: Simon & Schuster, 2000.

4

WEDDING/ PARTY PLANNER

An office Christmas party, an author's book launch, and a wedding actually have one thing in common: someone was probably hired to plan these events and execute them. The role of the event or party planner, a job title that didn't formally exist before 1990, has evolved over the past decade into one of the fastest-growing fields in the United

States. Party planning entails everything from making choices for corporate functions to personal parties. With so many decisions to make, more and more people hire a professional to help bring their dream event to life.

Description

Party and wedding planners usually operate out of small companies since a deep knowledge of local venues and vendors is essential to make an event successful. Some companies have their own staff to handle assignments, but most bring in outside experts.

Party planners must be experts in a wide variety of areas. They need to know where to hire entertainers and musicians, where to buy the right kind of food and flowers, and how best to let people know where and when the event is occurring.

The Web site About.com describes the skills required for a wedding planner—skills that apply to most other event planners as well: "A wedding planner must be able to remain calm in the face of adversity. Of course, he or she must be personable and ... [be] a good negotiator. You are the mouthpiece for the bride and groom when it comes to ordering flowers, hiring a band and photographer, finding a caterer, [and more]. You must be able to get them the best service for the lowest price—your reputation will depend on it. Networking is also important. Establishing good connections

This wedding planner discusses various celebration cakes with a young couple who are about to be married. Wedding planners usually offer a basic package to couples that can include hiring caterers, musicians, florists, bakers, designers, and more.

will help ensure that you get good deals. That's not all. Running your own business, as well as spending someone else's money, requires that you be adept at handling finances. You must also be very well organized."

Education and Training

A wedding or party planner must have a good design and fashion sense. He or she should know about color, music, and flowers. A good knowledge of religions is also important since wedding ceremonies are often religious. Party planners, and wedding planners in particular, should have detailed knowledge of many different types of cultural ceremonies. Keeping up with the latest trends is also vital.

Although a college degree is not required to be a party or wedding planner, basic business skills are always useful. Relevant courses in high school for prospective party

Kool Events

With her partner, Anne Morin, Amy Kool runs Kool Events, a New York City–based full-service planning service. "I'm an artist, Anne's a musician," Kool says in an interview. "When I graduated in the 1980s, I found there were [too few] jobs for artists . . . I ended up working in the entertainment field." Kool and her partner worked at various nightclubs for more than a decade. As Wall Street firms and other corporations expanded their businesses, there was a need for corporate planners.

"Companies wanted something different, fun things like theme parties, team-building events, networking, and client entertainment. I was involved with music, catering, entertainment, and coming up with ideas for different types of events.

"For us, it was great because we're creative people, my art background allowed me to look at a space and envision how it would look with the finished themes and party designs.

"One of my most favorite parties was for Ketchum Publishing. They were releasing a cookbook with recipes from markets of the world, so we turned the

(continued on page 46)

space into an international marketplace. People attending the author's book signing party got gold coins to purchase items at the booths."

"A client calls," Kool says of a typical event, "and we first get specifications including time, concept,

Theme parties are a huge draw for guests at public relations and press events. In this 2001 photograph with the event's co-cocoordinators, a table at the 73rd Annual Academy Awards Party is decked out in a tribute to the birth of motion pictures. The table's centerpiece is a zoetrope, an early motion picture device.

budget, and the number of people involved. We then find a location, plan a menu or work with the restaurant/venue, plan the event's schedule, and determine if there are giveaways [or favors]."

Once the client likes the proposal from Kool Events, they sign a contract and then the staff gets to work. Since they do not advertise, they rely entirely on referrals. After months of planning, Kool or members of her staff will arrive on site. Did the right food, flowers, decorations, and audio/visual equipment arrive on time? Is everything provided as planned?

Summing up, Kool identifies the traits a person needs to succeed in this field: "To do events [well] you need imagination, a knowledge of wines and foods, an understanding of how furniture fits into space, how to make things flow; you have to be a perfectionist. You have to be flexible since there's always a problem to handle. You have to be patient; you're dealing with human beings. You need good communication and writing skills. You have to be able to write down descriptions of events in a clear way; you have to be able to correspond with people; you have to have some command of the English language. You can't write a terrible proposal; it has to be literate."

planners include economics, marketing, creative writing, math, English, and art. The Web site iVillage.com estimates the following start-up costs should you decide to start your own planning business: $2,000 and up for a computer and software; $100 to $5,000 to market yourself via advertisements in the yellow pages, other local publications, and through direct-mail campaigns; $500 and up for your wardrobe. The vast majority of planners work from home offices, so rent is not a major issue.

Just about everything that is normally needed for a wedding can be applied to parties, which may range from a sweet-sixteen dance to a retirement function. Again, the planner tailors the event to the desires of its guest of honor and his or her friends and family, finding the best possible location, overall theme, menu, cake, decorations, and so on, down to the smallest details. The latest trend among event planners, according to a July 2005 *USA Today* article, is planning customized funerals. One noteworthy example was that of a passionate football fan who was embalmed, propped in his favorite recliner, and situated as if he were about to watch the weekend games.

Several consultants suggest volunteering with an established planner as a valuable way to evaluate how suited you are to the business and to make important contacts at the same time. Given the popularity of the field, some small companies receive upward of fifty résumés a week from people looking to get started. People who work for these firms usually start with minimum wage and work their way up based on their efficiency, communication, and social skills.

Salary

Fees charged by party and wedding planners are variable, which means your income is always changing. Typically, planners charge a fee of 10 to 15 percent of the cost of an event to organize and manage it. This means that your annual salary will vary greatly depending upon the amount of work you do, where you live, and how successful you are at planning events.

Outlook

Party and wedding planning is a new field, so available data is scant. However, jobs such as these are becoming more widespread. More and more individuals seem to be tapping into the skills of successful planners, not just brides and up-and-coming corporate types.

FOR MORE INFORMATION

ORGANIZATIONS

Association of Bridal Consultants
56 Danbury Road, Suite 11
New Milford, CT 06776
(860) 355-0464
Web site: http://www.bridalassn.com

International Special Events Society
401 N. Michigan Avenue
Chicago, IL 60611-4267
(800) 688-4737
Web site: http://www.ises.com

National Association of Catering Executives
9881 Broken Land Parkway, Suite 101
Columbia, MD 21046
(410) 290-5410
Web site: http://nace.net

TRADE SHOWS

The Special Event Conference and Trade Show (Annual)
(800) 927-5007
Web site: http://www.thespecialevent.com

WEB SITES

Business Know-How—Event and Party-Planning Business Start-Up Tools
http://www.businessknowhow.com/partyplanner

This Web site contains start-up tips and resources for event and party planners.

Event Solutions Magazine
http://www.event-solutions.com
> This electronic magazine contains ideas, solutions, and resources.

Party and Paper Retailer
http://www.partypaper.com
> This Web site contains valuable information about purchasing wholesale party supplies.

Special Events
http://www.specialevents.com
> This electronic magazine showcases articles by well-known event and party planners.

BOOKS

Roney, Carley. *The Knot Ultimate Wedding Planner: Worksheets, Checklists, Etiquette, Calendars, and Answers to Frequently Asked Questions.* New York, NY: Random House, 1999.
Tutera, David. *The Party Planner.* New York, NY: Bulfinch, 2005.

PERIODICALS

Special Events
17383 Sunset Boulevard, Suite A220
Pacific Palisades, CA 90272
(800) 543-4116
Web site: http://www.specialevents.com
> This magazine contains a variety of resources related to event and party planning.

5

EVENT COORDINATOR

Event coordinator and party planner are similar careers that encompass many of the same tasks. Event coordinators, however, tend to work on a larger scale and almost exclusively do work for corporations. For example, there is approximately $80 billion a year spent on these events according to the Professional Conference Management Association.

Description

The Department of Labor estimates there are 34,000 event planners in the United States. They break the field into three sections: "In workplaces with several meeting planners, three levels of professionalism exist: the facilitator, the technician, and the professional. The facilitator may be assigned basic tasks such as choosing menus and working with the hotel on a variety of details. A person holding this position is concerned with the physical needs of the attendees. The technician is often responsible for running registration

Working as an event planner often involves the coordination of many people and companies such as florists, bakeries, decorators, musicians, entertainers, and caterers, such as the women featured in this photograph.

and reservations, selecting and setting up the site, and operating the budget. The professional designs and sells the event, creates the budget, and oversees all operations. It is this top-level manager who is responsible for achieving the meeting's overall objective: the communication goal of the client."

What is an event? It could be the halftime show at the Super Bowl or it could be an off-site training session for corporate managers. It usually involves a special occasion, away from the office, and quite often involves the general public.

Planning and budgeting for these events usually takes weeks, if not months, involving invitations, advertising, visiting various sites, arranging for meals or staffing, and figuring out the entertainment and other creative ways to effectively communicate the client's message. Many of these events mean interfacing with counterparts at the site, or with people in related fields such as catering, florists, media communications, and corporate officials.

When an event is needed, perhaps the company picnic or the introduction of a new product, the in-house planners are consulted. For many companies, they turn to independent planning companies to handle the arrangements. At the first meeting, the parameters of the event are outlined, including such details as the timing and location.

The first thing the event coordinator is likely to do is check the calendars of the major corporate officers to make sure they are free and clear to attend. If the event is a product launch, the event coordinator needs to ensure that that product is on schedule. If a space is needed, one is located and reserved. Once the space is chosen, the rest of the arrangements can follow. The coordinator may be required to establish a guest list, determine if registration is needed, and if so, how to process that information (by phone, mail, fax, or Internet).

To handle all of the details, the coordinator must be good at record keeping and financial negotiating, and have excellent communication skills. Because he or she is the intermediary between the company and all of the vendors providing the various services that will support the event, courteous and responsive communication is extremely important. Creative thinking will be required in making an initial presentation to a client. Creativity also comes into play when making the event come to life and when inevitable problems occur. The coordinator's job can be hectic and noisy, and filled with long days, especially as the event date looms, many of which will be spent with a cell phone in hand at all times.

Education and Training

To prepare for a career as an event coordinator, your high school courses should include English, business, speech, and a foreign language. Summer jobs working in the hospitality industry—at hotels, restaurants, and resorts—will also help. Other possibilities to gain related experience might be found by volunteering at your local office of tourism. Once in the field, you should get certified through the organization

Michael T. Fiur Productions

Michael T. Fiur had no idea his career would lead him to work as a producer. After graduating from college, he stayed in Binghamton, New York, to organize a mayoral race, which he helped win, and then served on the mayor's staff. The hurly-burly lifestyle and

This screenshot is part of the Web site of producer and event planner Michael T. Fiur, whose company's client list includes the United States Tennis Association, the National Football League, and the Alliance for a New Humanity.

constant planning of events over six years inspired him to become a large-scale event coordinator/producer.

President of Michael T. Fiur Productions, Fiur is a leading producer of events in the United States. After leaving politics, he moved home to New York City and began working with Madison Square Garden's entertainment division before starting a ten-year stint at Radio City Music Hall. While there, he worked on five Super Bowl halftime shows, six productions of the Radio City Christmas Spectacular, and numerous corporate and civic events. All that experience inspired him to form his own company. His experience also landed the contracts to produce Arthur Ashe Kids' Day each year and all the entertainment for the U.S. Open. Fiur is currently developing an off-Broadway musical called *Superstar*.

"As a live event/television and theatrical producer, I view my role as the 'glue' that holds it all together," he explains. "I am responsible for managing the budget, hiring the creative team, overseeing the creative process, holding the client's hand, and seeing the show through to successful completion. My two rules of producing are to create a truly memorable experience for the audience, and stay on budget."

Meeting Professionals International, which is listed in the directory at the end of this chapter.

Corporations, hotels, and convention centers often have their own planning staffs as well as employees from private companies that provide similar services. As a result, once you enter the event-planning field, there are many opportunities to learn, and possibly some to advance your career. Employees can advance to positions in management, quite often being promoted from within, or drafted from one company to another. Recruiting is a standard practice in event-planning fields. Cross-recruiting may also bring people to travel companies and museums.

To start in the field, try for an internship at places such as convention bureaus and exhibition centers to gain experience. The Department of Labor notes, however, that "although experience can be gained by arranging weddings and catering parties for acquaintances or family members, this type of experience alone is rarely sufficient to be hired as a corporate meeting planner without having a broader work history in event planning and obtaining certification." There is also a growing field of course work at colleges in hotel management programs for people who want to learn more about the business. Once in the field, successful planners attend annual seminars, workshops, conventions, and trade meetings while also reading trade journals and browsing Web sites to stay ahead of trends.

Leslie Taylor, event coordinator for the Cocoa Beach Chamber of Commerce, holds a replica of a prop used in the television show *I Dream of Jeannie*. She organized a fortieth anniversary event of the show's first episode for Cocoa Beach's 13,000 residents.

Salary

Starting salaries for event coordinators are usually between $28,000 and $30,000. According to the Department of Labor, the average salary for event planners in 2000 was $54,600. Meeting Planners International released a western regional salary survey report in 2000. It showed that corporate planners' salaries were slightly higher, with the average being $59,800. According to the same report, religious planners' earnings fell at the bottom of the scale at $38,500.

Outlook

Event coordinators and planners may work in both the public and private sectors. In the long term, opportunities in the event-planning fields are available and growing. In the past decade, more and more corporations have outsourced their event-planning and promotional needs to independent contractors. Event coordinators might be hired by a variety of firms including hotel chains, educational institutions, corporations, convention centers, municipal parks, and tourism associations. In addition, many event coordinators with experience can cross over into a host of related careers such as those in public relations, hospitality management, or even organizing the catering and social functions of film and television production companies.

FOR MORE INFORMATION

ORGANIZATIONS

Convention Industry Council
8201 Greensboro Drive, Suite 300
McLean, VA 22102
(800) 725-8982
Web site: http://www.conventionindustry.org

Meeting Professionals International
4455 LBJ Freeway, Suite 1200
Dallas, TX 75244-5903
(972) 702-3000
Web site: http://www.mpiweb.org

WEB SITES

Event Planner—A National Internet Resource for Event Planning
http://www.event-planner.com/
   This Web site is a national resource for event planning resources.

Event Planner.com
http://www.eventplanner.com/
   This is a professional Web site that lists a variety of resources,
   including employment boards.

Event Planning Tips
http://www.librarysupport.net/librarylovers/eventips.html
   This Web site hosts a comprehensive article about careers in event
   planning.

BOOKS

Allen, Judy. *The Business of Event Planning: Behind-the-Scenes Secrets of Successful Special Events.* Hoboken, NJ: John Wiley & Sons, 2002.

Allen, Judy. *Event Planning: The Ultimate Guide to Successful Meetings, Corporate Events, Fundraising Galas, Conferences, Conventions, Incentives and Other Special Events.* Hoboken, NJ: John Wiley & Sons, 2000.

Camenson, Blythe. *Opportunities in Event Planning Careers.* New York, NY: McGraw-Hill, 2002.

Turner, Krista. *Start Your Own Event Planning Business: Your Step-by-Step Guide to Success.* Irvine, CA: Entrepreneur Press, 2004.

PERIODICALS

Event Solutions
5400 Lakeshore Drive, Suite 101
Tempe, AZ 85283
(480) 831-5100
Web site: http://www.event-solutions.com/
　　This magazine provides a variety of resources for established wedding planners, including vendors, contacts, and other resources.

The Meeting Professional
3030 LBJ Freeway, Suite 1700
Dallas, TX 75234-2759
(972) 702-3000
Web site: http://www.mpiweb.org/
　　This is the magazine of Meeting Professionals International (MPI), the global authority and resource for the meeting industry.

6

TRADE-SHOW ORGANIZER

Trade-show organizers either work for organizations that run trade shows for different corporations, or they work directly for facilities to attract business. There are many different titles that are offshoots of a career in organizing trade shows, such as conference and meeting planner, conference planner, conference services

Trade-show organizers have the exhausting task of coordinating the needs of hundreds and sometimes thousands of exhibitors and their displays. This is a bird's eye view of one such event: the Comdex computer trade show in Las Vegas, Nevada.

officer, convention coordinator, event planner, festival organizer, meeting planner, special-events organizer, or trade-show planner.

Description

The California Department of Labor notes, "Planners on a large staff for associations and convention bureaus may be assigned one specific aspect of the event such as budgeting or handling reservations and registration, while planners who work for smaller organizations will often take responsibility for all phases of the event.

"The massive logistical operation of a large convention, trade show, or expo often starts as many as five years before the event. The first step, booking space in halls and hotels, often must be done years in advance. Then, one or two years before the event, meeting planners begin developing topics, choosing featured speakers, and creating agendas. Much of the work also involves coordinating with other organizations and companies who will present programs and set up booths. Sometimes hundreds of vendors will exhibit their services or products."

Expoweb.com provides a list of responsibilities for trade-show organizers, although not every position requires people to do everything on the list. Conference and event planners perform some or all of the following duties:

- Meet with trade and professional associations and other groups to promote and discuss conference, convention, and trade-show services
- Meet with sponsors and organizing committees to plan the scope of events, to establish and monitor budgets, and to review administrative procedures and progress
- Coordinate services for events, such as accommodation and transportation for participants, conference and other facilities, catering, signage, displays, translations,

special needs requirements, audio-visual equipment, printing, and security

- Organize registration of participants, prepare programs and promotional materials, and publicize events through local advertisers
- Plan entertainment and social gatherings for participants
- Hire, train, and supervise support staff required for events
- Ensure compliance with required laws
- Negotiate contracts for services, approve suppliers' invoices, maintain financial records, review final billing submitted to clients for events, and prepare reports

Just about every show takes years to plan, whether it's a first-time or a recurring event. The first step is booking the space. This part can be tricky, especially if the event continues to attract new attendees each year. A space that's too small can kill potential business by overcrowding people and distracting them with too much noise. If a space is too large, the opposite can happen: the vendors and businesses seem paltry and attendance might further decrease. In some cases, the location can expand to accommodate more people, but not every venue has this luxury. Locating a suitable space requires an exact understanding of the client's needs. How much space should be allocated for individual booths? How should booths be spaced apart to accommodate discussions? Will there be an area reserved for food and refreshments? Is there an area needed for registering participants or attendants? Will there be promotional giveaways, a raffle, or other items, such as a guide to the various booths, handed out to attendees? All of these questions and more have to be addressed during the early planning stage.

Once all of these needs are assessed, a suitable space can be reserved. Then a layout of booths is done, and work begins on attracting vendors to display their wares. In many cases, vendors buy booth space at predetermined prices that are based on location. Returning vendors normally get their pick of location and can even receive discounts on the price. Even so, about 40 percent of the vendors miss their critical deadlines, which forces the organizer to keep in touch to make sure everyone is in compliance and steady progress is being made.

The trade-show event staff has to work with the customer to advertise the event within the trade—sometimes both locally and nationally—and then make sure they are equipped to handle first the vendors arriving with their booths and equipment, and then the attendees who need to be registered. Planners tend to also be involved in travel arrangements for various participants, so a good familiarity with the Internet is a must. Planners must also comply with the Americans with Disabilities Act, since trade shows are required by law to offer access for disabled people. While

GETS FUN

WHERE BUSINESS

E3

entertainment
software
association

this may sound simple, a typical booth usually requires its own equipment that needs union crews to assemble, providing it with light, power, phone lines, and Internet connections. Planners must also ensure that each booth meets state fire regulations and that any person, with a disability or not, can enter and exit without trouble. The problems that can come up with the registration process alone are enough to raise the blood pressure of the most sedate trade-show coordinator, so it is a must that he or she be able to keep things running smoothly while under pressure.

Education and Training

A potential trade-show organizer must be excellent at managing his or her time. He or she must also be proficient with a variety of basic software programs, so taking computer classes in high school is a must. Volunteer and community service work will also help prepare you for this type of career. More than anything else, you must enjoy working with people and the challenges that often come up when trying to organize a large event.

A worker passes a display for the Entertainment Software Association, one of the exhibitors in the Electronic Entertainment Exposition, which was held in the Los Angeles Convention Center in 2005. Trade-show organizers must work with a team of audio and video engineers in order to provide consumers with an engaging promotional experience.

Salary

A salary survey conducted by Meeting Planners International and published in the May 2000 *Meeting Manager* magazine shows the average yearly salaries for people in the field:

Corporate Planners	$59,800
Association Planners	$47,800
Independent Planners	$63,100
University Planners	$38,300
Government Planners	$45,000
Religious Planners	$38,500

To perform this job well, people need to have good communications skills, both verbal and written. They also need to be ready to handle multiple problems at the same time.

Outlook

According to statistics from the market research company VNU, there were approximately 4,900 trade and consumer shows planned for the United States and Canada in 2005. More than 1.2 million companies exhibited new products and services to more than 50 million people at these shows. Each of the nearly 5,000 shows required planning, organization, and publicity.

Careers in trade-show organizing are expected to continue growing. Many municipalities are planning convention or exhibition centers as part of revitalization plans for their communities. On any given day, there are multiple trade shows in major cities around the United States serving a variety of business professionals.

Sam Bundy, group president for VNU Exposition's ASD/AMD Merchandise Group, sees the trade-show field as a vibrant opportunity for young people. One of the areas he feels is strongly suited for starters is customer service/telemarketing. These are the people who "contact prior attendees of trade shows to facilitate customer needs by providing information and pre-registering them for the next event," Bundy says. They also field inbound inquiries for information and/or convention service needs.

For this entry-level position, Bundy stresses that people need good verbal skills, the ability to multitask, a strong work ethic, and the ability to handle a heavy volume of incoming calls while entering data.

"This starter position is an incubator by providing a platform to learn the business and market," Bundy adds. "Future opportunities are in show operations or sales. I have six

Individual workers assemble dozens of exhibits for the Electronic Entertainment Exposition in preparation for the annual trade-show about consumer electronics. Because retailers often demonstrate new products at these trade shows, almost every exhibit has to be electrically wired.

employees who started out as customer service representatives who are now in sales or operations. Two of them are senior level managers."

Getting in isn't difficult, and registering with local temporary employment agencies is a good start, Bundy continues. He got into the business through such an agency, and at his Las Vegas show, for example, hired fifty temporary staff members. To find a position, Bundy suggests contacting the human resources departments at trade-show management companies, checking out the Internet employment sites for the companies, or joining one of the associations for the field. Depending on experience and location, Bundy notes these positions pay $30,000 to $40,000 a year.

FOR MORE INFORMATION

ORGANIZATIONS

Convention Industry Council
8201 Greensboro Drive, Suite 300
McLean, VA 22102
(800) 725-8982
Web site: http://www.conventionindustry.org

Exhibit Designers and Producers Association (EDPA)
5775 Peachtree-Dunwoody Road
Building G, Suite 500
Atlanta, GA 30342
(404) 303-7310
Web site: http://www.edpa.com

International Association of Convention and Visitors Bureaus
2025 M Street NW, Suite 500
Washington, DC 20036
(202) 296-7888
Web site: http://www.iacvb.org

Meeting Professionals International (MPI)
4455 LBJ Freeway, Suite 1200
Dallas, TX 75244-5903

(972) 702-3000
Web site: http://www.mpiweb.org

CERTIFICATION PROGRAMS

Trade Fair Certification Program
U.S. Department of Commerce
14th & Constitution Avenue NW, Room 2116
Washington, DC 20230
(202) 482-2525
Web site: http://www.export.gov/comm_svc/trade_fair_
certification.html

WEB SITES

Exhibitor Online
http://www.exhibitoronline.com
This Web site contains nearly everything a potential trade-show organizer needs to know about trade-show and corporate event marketing.

Expo Web: Intelligence, Insight, and Ideas for Convention and Trade-Show Professionals
http://www.expoweb.com
This Web site contains information about strategies and solutions for successful trade shows.

International Association for Exhibition Management
http://www.iaem.org
This Web site contains information about joining this important industry association.

Trade Show Specialist—Trade-Show Resources
http://ga.tradeshowspecialist.com
This Web site contains a comprehensive list of Internet resources related to organizing trade shows.

Trade Show Week—**An Electronic Magazine**
http://tradeshowweek.com
   This is an electronic magazine devoted to industry professionals.

BOOKS

Arnold, Marlys K. *Build a Better Trade Show Image*. Kansas City, MO: Tiffany Harbor Productions, 2002.

Lynn, Jim. *Trade Show Gymnastics: Jumping Through Hoops Without Getting Hurt*. Ann Arbor, MI: Fairview Studios Publications, 1998.

Miller, Steve. *How to Get the Most Out of Trade Shows*. New York, NY: McGraw-Hill. 2000.

Morrow, Sandra. *The Art of the Show: An Introduction to the Study of Exposition Management*. Dallas, TX: IAEM Foundation, 2001.

PERIODICALS

EXPO
11600 College Boulevard
Overland Park, KS 66210
(913) 469-1185
Web site: http://www.expoweb.com
   Almost everything a trade-show organizer needs to know is contained in this magazine.

Trade Show Executive **magazine**
701 Palomar Airport Road, Suite 300
Carlsbad, CA 92009
(760) 931-4857
Web site: http://www.tradeshowexecutive.com
   This publication is the premiere journal for professional trade-show organizers.

7

PROFESSIONAL ORGANIZER

Some people see a cluttered desk or a stuffed closet and wish they could figure out how to simplify their mess. Others see the problem and immediately know how to best get things under control. It's those people who may find a career as a professional organizer.

Accountemps, a temporary staffing service, conducted a survey and concluded that corporate executives waste five weeks of each year trying to locate missing items. Homeowners probably spend as much, if not more, time doing the same thing.

Description

A professional organizer is usually hired by corporate executives or homeowners to help them solve their immediate clutter problems as well as teach them strategies to help keep the problems from repeating. He or she will arrive at the workplace or home, assess the problem, discuss an approach, and then set to work. Sometimes organizational problems can be solved in a single day, but most problems that require a professional need several days if not weeks to get under control.

Among the most overwhelming symptoms of a person who suffers from chronic clutter is hoarding a tremendous amount of papers, receipts, bills, taxes, and other personal documents. Many people who choose a career as a professional organizer will be faced with sorting through—or helping his or her client sort through—years of personal records.

An organizer will concentrate on controlling clutter, helping to develop filing systems for paperwork, important documents, photographs, and media. Other personal items such as clothing, cosmetics, linens, and collectibles also need to be made orderly. Personal organizers can examine an existing space and help maximize its potential, creating a personalized storage system that suits the client's lifestyle.

The Web site Organizedtimes.com points out, "Regardless of their background, all successful 'veteran' organizers share certain characteristics—a passion for organizing principles, a strong set of people skills, the ability to teach new ideas to people, sharply honed 'problem-solving' skills, and the ability to organize their own business dealings. But don't worry if you feel you're lacking in some of these areas—becoming an organizer is a continual process of growing, so you will acquire these skills as you evolve."

Education and Training

As of now, there are few organizations offering certification for this profession. The National Association of Professional Organizers (NAPO) has spent eight years researching the situation and developing guidelines with a certification program to be initiated in 2007. Until then, professional organizers have to make their work stand out each time, so word of mouth will provide the reputation required to achieve the next assignment.

Professional organizers usually have a system of filing that they teach their clients as part of their attempt to help them get control over their clutter. Getting work experience as an office filer can help you learn excellent skills in this area.

Many long-established companies, including the NAPO, offer training services. These courses can be taught in class-rooms, conferences, and even via the Internet. Fees are required and some firms will require first-timers to take their classes before being hired. Some of the topics covered include business basics such as:

- Should I charge a project fee?
- Should I charge different amounts for consultations and hands-on work?

- Should I offer a free consultation?
- Who pays for traveling costs?
- When and how should I get paid?
- What do I need to know about preparing proposals for professional work?
- How do I market my services to individuals and corporations?

Additionally, some organizers suggest taking supplemental college or adult-school classes at nearby schools in financial management, writing a business plan, general business, and basic marketing.

Organizations such as the NAPO offer seminars and conferences throughout the year. They also hold a national meeting that rotates locations in different regions throughout the country from year to year. (The 2007 meeting is set for Minneapolis.)

Salary

Experienced organizers tend to charge an hourly fee in the $45 to $65 range according to Organizedtimes.com. During the first meeting, the job is assessed and a plan is created. At that point, an estimate for the number of hours involved is discussed, as well as for materials that are required (storage bins, file folders, and whatever may be bought new or acquired from the homeowner to accomplish the goal). Once the client accepts the estimate, some organizers ask for a deposit to guarantee a level of commitment from the client. Based on the number of clients taken on, organizers can earn as little as $500 a month to four times that amount or more.

One such organizer, Ann Gambrell, told *Working World* magazine, "Your fee depends on experience. Remember, you are changing someone's life. Some can charge upwards of hundreds of dollars an hour. But most beginners are asking from $25 to $35 an hour. In a few years you can get that to $60, $70, and more, depending on where you live in the country." It's noted by many that fees for work in private homes tend to be less than fees for corporate offices. Many organizers maintain separate fee scales for both.

Getting the word out is an important part of the profession. California-based organizing business the Busy Woman's Daily Planner uses the following advertising methods:

- Direct mailings twice per year
- E-mailings two to three times per year
- Phone calls six times per year at minimum
- Donating "organizing time" as a promotion
- Coupons in "mom" packs, put in orders, or handed out
- Advertisements at trade shows and conventions

Jennifer Pacifico, who has run her own organizing business, Wings 4 Organizing, LLC, for seventeen years, offers the following advice: "Be consistent. Have great-looking professionally made business cards and avoid a cookie-cutter mentality. Clients are different, and their organizational needs vary a lot from one to the other."

Outlook

The NAPO says that 94 percent of its members are women, mostly working part-time. The field has experienced explosive growth since the mid-1990s. The media has helped promote the field, too, since professional organizers are now being showcased on programs on the Learning Channel and Home & Garden Television. Barry Izsak, president of the NAPO, told Web site Mysanantonio.com, "In all honesty, getting organized isn't rocket science. What we usually see as the reason that people need help is that they feel overwhelmed. A professional organizer helps them step back, look at the situation, analyze it and unlock the mystery, and helps them create a process." In many cases, the victims of clutter are people who have unusual attachments to unnecessary items like books, magazines, and newspapers. Other people are just natural collectors who have stepped over the line from manageable to unlivable. Since Americans live in such a consumer-driven culture, the need for personal organizers will likely increase in the next decade. Now is the perfect time to get in on this emerging field.

FOR MORE INFORMATION

ORGANIZATIONS

National Association of Professional Organizers (NAPO)
4700 W. Lake Avenue
Glenview, IL 60025
(847) 375-4746
Web site: http://napo.net

National Association of Professional Organizers
Los Angeles Chapter
10573 Pico Boulevard
Los Angeles, CA 90064
(213) 487-4477
Web site: http://www.napola.org

National Association of Professional Organizers
Washington, DC, Chapter
P.O. Box 7301
Arlington, VA 22207-0301
(202) 362-6276
Web site: http://www.dcorganizers.org

Professional Organizers
255 Dundas Street West
P.O. Box 82032
Waterdown, ON L0R 2M0
Canada
(416) 778-5371
Web site: http://www.organizersincanada.com

TRAINING & CERTIFICATE PROGRAMS
Certificate Program in Professional Organizing
National Study Group on Chronic Disorganization (NSGCD)
P.O. Box 1990
Elk Grove, CA 95759
(916) 962-6227
Web site: http://www.nsgcd.org

The HG Training Academy
1591 Yarnell Street, #188
Sylmar, CA 91342
(818) 686-8888
Web site: http://www.professional-organizers.com

WEB SITES
Organized Living
http://www.organized-living.com
This Web site is devoted to helping people remain organized and it contains hundreds of related tips and ideas.

Organizing Network
http://www.myorganizedlife.com
This is another Web site that contains ideas for how to organize a person's life and his or her stuff.

Time to Organize
http://www.time2organize.net
This is the electronic component to the print newsletter with tips on how to become a professional organizer.

BOOKS
Eisenburg, Ronni. *Organize Your Office! Simple Routines for Managing Your Workspace*. New York, NY: Hyperion Press, 1999.

Glovinsky, Cindy. *One Thing at a Time: 100 Simple Ways to Live Clutter-Free Every Day*. New York, NY: St. Martin's Press, 2004.

Morgenstern, Julie. *Organizing from the Inside Out*. New York, NY: Owl Books, 1998.

Smallin, Donna. *Organizing Plain and Simple: A Ready Reference Guide with Hundreds of Solutions to Your Everyday Clutter Challenges*. North Adams, MA: Storey Publishing, 2002.

Steinbacher, Lisa. *The Professional Organizer's Complete Business Guide*. St. Paul, MN: Eternity Publishing, 2004.

Waddill, Kathy. *The Organizing Sourcebook: Nine Strategies For Organizing Your Life*. New York, NY: McGraw Hill, 2001.

PERIODICALS

Home

1633 Broadway
New York, NY 10019
Web site: http://www.homemag.com/

This is a wonderful magazine for the do-it-yourself person who is searching for home improvement project resources.

Simple Living

P.O. Box 2060
Forrester Center, WV 25438-9954
Web site: http://wwwsimpleliving.com/

This consumer magazine has a variety of tips on how to stay organized and clutter-free.

8

LIFE COACH

Just as there are people who look in a closet and can't imagine how to clear the clutter, there are some who look at their lives and want to improve them, but have no idea how to do it. Some people turn to a life coach for assistance. This is a person who makes a career out of offering confused people a fresh, objective perspective, and often a serious examination and assessment of his or her client's choices and future.

Description

A life coach needs to be able to listen to a person's goals and aspirations, understand the obstacles the client imagines exist, and then work with him or her to lift the obstacles and chart a course for personal fulfillment. Life coaches work with people in all walks of life, in different professions and circumstances. As a result, a life coach needs to understand not just the person and his or her personal circumstances, but the career to which he or she aspires. Unlike a professional organizer, a life coach works with concrete facts as well as spiritual and philosophical issues, so the word "coach" is entirely appropriate.

Coachlink.net describes the life coach profession as follows: "Coaching integrates principles from the fields of education, psychology, business, and personal transformation. Your coach serves as your personal consultant, partner, sounding board, and confidante, championing you to improve your effectiveness and achieve your goals. Your coach partners with you to improve your focus, to hold yourself accountable, and celebrate your successes."

In the best-case scenario, life coaches will help their clients develop their natural abilities and channel those into a rewarding career. Life coaching, however, is not therapy. If

Reggie Adams, a life coach who works out of her home office, is seen in this 2004 photograph on the telephone with one of her clients. Many life coaches begin as executives. In their spare time, many help their peers make career choices or deal with life changes.

a client requires the assistance of a psychologist, psychotherapist, or psychiatrist, then he or she should seek that help immediately. Unlike close friends or associates, life coaches can objectively zero in on their clients' career and job experience. A life coach outlines a person's good and bad points in a truthful way and teaches a client methods to accentuate the positive.

Businessballs.com, a reference source for corporate executives, notes, "[Life] coaching is a relatively new and different profession—different [from] psychology, counseling, or therapy. The big difference between coaching and counseling is that coaching doesn't claim to have the answers. A coach's job is not to go over old ground, be past-orientated, or to force-feed information, but to work with clients *to help them find the answers themselves."*

Andrea Howard, an employment counselor with the New York State Department of Labor, explains, "[Life] coaches help define goals and obtain excellence. The job search process can be tough on the self-esteem. Repeated rejections can be discouraging. Coaches offer support, motivation, and encouragement. Coaches listen to detect thoughts, feelings, and aspirations related to career decision-making. They also ask questions and provide feedback on clients' strengths, insecurities, concerns, areas of need, and career-related obstacles. They help clients develop goals and achieve a higher level of performance and satisfaction."

The coaching process can occur in person or by phone, but less often by e-mail. Some arrangements blend all three, although coaches tend to prefer one method or another. A person seeking a life coach needs to make a commitment of time since a single session only identifies the problem. Normally, life coaches look for a three-month plan, some as many as six months.

Life coaches will tell you that they are not miracle workers and the client must be willing to use the advice and

One of the aspects of being a life coach is examining a client's résumé. As a professional and promotional tool, a person's résumé needs to provide the most essential, updated information about his or her professional experience in an attractive, concise format. Many people, including executives, find preparing a résumé daunting.

implement it. A successful coach will provide a clear plan for achieving the identified goals, teach you skills to put the plan into action, and help find ways to keep you focused. If successful, the lessons taught by a coach can last a person the rest of his or her life.

Education and Training

Many of the lessons imparted by life coaches may appear to be common sense, but he or she has to find ways to communicate in terms the client will comprehend and accept. For would-be coaches, there are many private companies willing to teach you those methods for a price. The entire field is not regulated or tracked by the federal government, so standards vary from company to company.

There are two organizations that offer certification, each subscribing to a code of ethics and practices. There are many other organizations for life coaches in this still-growing field. Most companies suggest that life coaches have experience in other fields, too, and bring those experiences to bear when helping others. Some organizations such as Coachlink insist that their coaches have also been clients so they understand the other side of the process.

Salary

Once selected by a client, the coach then outlines the schedule of meetings, method of meeting, and an estimate for the duration of the relationship. From there a fee structure is outlined and an agreement is usually made between coach and client.

The fee structure will vary. Usually, a life coach may earn at least $300 for six forty-five-minute sessions, either conducted in person or on the telephone. Subsequent sessions will vary depending on the agreed-upon pricing structure.

Outlook

While it is extremely difficult to estimate the future job market for a relatively new career such as that of life coach, chances are that it represents a growing market. With the sheer number of career decisions that people of all ages and backgrounds are faced with today, and the fact that many careers are no longer lifelong vocations, the average person embarks on a variety of different careers in his or her lifetime.

With such frequent change, life coaches are likely to be contacted by increasing clients in the future. Other economic situations might influence and increase the demand for life coaches including more prevalent corporate consolidations and lay-offs, changing technologies, and the decrease in domestic manufacturing jobs due to the phenomenon of globalization.

FOR MORE INFORMATION

ORGANIZATIONS

International Coach Federation
2365 Harrodsburg Road, Suite A325
Lexington, KY 40504
(888) 423-3131
Web site: http://www.coachfederation.org

The International Consortium for Coaching in Organizations
Agnes Mura, Chair
9912 Business Park Drive, Suite 170
Sacramento, CA 95827
(310) 450-5035
Web site: http://www.coachingconsortium.org

Worldwide Association of Business Coaches
8578 Echo Place West
Sidney, BC V8L 5E2
Canada
Web site: http://www.wabccoaches.com

WEB SITES

The Professional Coaches and Mentors Association
http://www.pcmaonline.com
> This Web site includes a calendar of events, directory, and other resources.

The Solution Box
http://www.solutionbox.com
> This is a great Web site for potential life coaches to get them thinking about questions and situations to speak about with clients.

BOOKS

Covey, Stephen R. *The Seven Habits of Highly Effective People*. New York, NY: Free Press, 2004.

Brown-Volkman, Deborah. *Four Steps to Building a Profitable Coaching Practice: A Complete Marketing Resource Guide for Coaches*. New York, NY: iUniverse, 2003.

Fairley, Stephen G., and Chris E. Stout. *Getting Started in Personal and Executive Coaching: How to Create a Thriving Coaching Practice*. Hoboken, NJ: John Wiley & Sons, 2003.

Martin, Curly. *The Life Coaching Handbook*. New York, NY: Crown Publishing, 2001.

OPERATIONS MANAGER

Just about everything that is manufactured for sale is composed of many parts. The organization of those parts—acquiring them, assembling them, and making them available for sale—requires coordination. In different fields, this job title is known as either trafficker, or more commonly, operations manager.

Description

Operations managers are the secret engines to successful companies. They ensure that businesses run smoothly. They establish schedules, projecting when fresh materials will be required. They also coordinate the shipping of materials and can handle production schedules, human resource schedules, and many other functions that keep companies on track. Some of the positions that fall under the field of operations management include assembly-line workers, mailroom operations, supply-chain managers, and much more. Operations professionals understand how each department is just one cog in the wheel of a larger corporation. They are people who work behind the scenes making sure that each area of a corporation functions as well as it can.

When looking at companies for work, study how they're organized. You'll find that each one has one or more departments dedicated to communication between departments, shipping and receiving goods, and making things run as smoothly as possible. The entry-level positions are usually clerical or assistant managers, responsible for a small piece of the puzzle. As people gain experience, they gain greater responsibility for the overall operation of the company. Senior operations people tend to be part of senior management. They are normally involved in decisions, such as where the

Dale Frederick *(left)*, operations manager at American Seafoods Processing in New Bedford, Massachusetts, takes a tour group through the scallop processing line. Operations managers are responsible for overseeing all stages of production in any business.

company is based, how facilities should be constructed or modified, and how new technologies can be integrated to improve workflow and production.

The operations department is vital to any company. Operations managers usually bear the brunt of some tedious work, with long hours and many problems that need immediate solving. Operations is an all-encompassing term, which, depending upon the size and scope of the company, may include positions in customer service, sales, accounting, logistics, production, and maintenance. Operations managers exist to support the company and its goals to produce the best possible goods in the shortest possible time. This can mean adjusting work schedules or finding better vendors for supplies.

Education and Training

While some companies may seek employees with business degrees or even MBA (master of business administration) degrees, many will hire people in the lower ranks if they can prove they have the problem-solving skills and personality to handle challenges. Once employed, skill and experience will make up for what is taught in classes. The skills usually sought for this position include not only an understanding of processes, but of people. Operations managers need to demonstrate strong leadership, sharp analytical skills, and excellent communications skills, both written and verbal. Another key element is building a team that can follow directions and work toward a common goal. Operations managers always work with a team, so good interpersonal skills are vital. High school students should take courses in English, math, computers, and even public speaking.

Salary

Salaries in the field of operations management vary by region, profession, and job title, so averages can fall anywhere between $18,000 for an entry-level position to $60,000 and

Ciro Viento, operations manager for Automated Waste Disposal, demonstrates a global positioning system that is used by the company to track workers and their vehicles in Connecticut. The satellite tracking system has saved the company thousands of dollars in overtime salaries.

up for a senior-level position. Most operations managers start as hourly employees and move into salaried positions through promotion. Also, since most operations people are promoted from within the company, it's a career that promises greater advancement than other jobs surveyed in this book. The Virginia Department of Labor says, "Career success is both about what you do (applying your technical knowledge, skills, and ability) and how you do it (the consistent behaviors you demonstrate and choose to use) while interacting and communicating with others."

Outlook

The field of operations management is seen as a growing one given the challenges companies face through increased international competition. With changing technology as well as the evolving marketplace, operations managers will succeed by staying on top of these changes as they pertain to their chosen profession. According to the U.S. Bureau of Labor, projected employment growth for top-level operations managers varies by industry; however, keen competition is expected for these positions because the prestige and high pay attract a large number of qualified applicants.

FOR MORE INFORMATION

ORGANIZATIONS

American Management Association
1601 Broadway
New York, NY 10019
(212) 586-8100
Web site: http://www.amanet.org

Association for Operations Management
5301 Shawnee Road
Alexandria, VA 22312-2317
(800) 444-2742
Web site: http://www.apics.org

Institute of Certified Professional Managers (ICPM)
James Madison University
MSC 5504
Harrisonburg, VA 22807
(800) 586-4120
Web site: http://cob.jmu.edu/icpm

National Management Association
2210 Arbor Boulevard
Dayton, OH 45439
(937) 294-0421
Web site: http://www.nma1.org

Production Operations Management Society (POMS)
College of Business, Florida International University
Miami, FL 33174
(305) 348-1413
Web site: http://www.poms.org

WEB SITES

Occupational Information Network—Operations Managers
http://online.onetcenter.org/link/summary/11-1021.00
This Web site provides a comprehensive look at careers in operations management.

BOOKS

Chase, Richard B., et al. *Operations Management for Competitive Advantage with Student-CD*. New York, NY: McGraw-Hill/Irwin, 2003.
Krajewski, Lee J., and Larry P. Ritzman. *Operations Management: Strategy and Analysis*. New York, NY: Prentice Hall Press, 2001.
Reid, Dan R., and Nada R. Sanders. *Operations Management: An Integrated Approach*. Hoboken, NJ: John Wiley & Sons, 2005.

Terwiesch, Cachon. *Matching Supply with Demand: An Introduction to Operations Management.* New York, NY: McGraw-Hill/Irwin, 2005.

Wallace, Thomas F. *Sales & Operations Planning: The How-to Handbook.* Portland, OR: T. F. Wallace & Co., 2004.

PERIODICALS

Manufacturing & Service Operations Management
Columbia Business School
3022 Broadway
412 Uris Hall
New York, NY 10027
(212) 854-4280
Web site: http://www.msom.org
This is the most well-known journal in the operations management industry.

10

MERCHANDISE PLANNER/ ASSISTANT PLANNER

As mentioned in chapter three, careers in retail sales can offer great organizing opportunities. However, most retail sales operations have employees called merchandise planners who determine the perfect product mix to place in each store, help figure out from which vendors to buy goods, and strategize how to maximize regional differences for optimum sales.

Description

The merchandise planner is responsible for developing an initial financial strategy for sales, markdowns, and profit. He or she has to project into the future and make an educated guess about what people will want to buy in specific product categories, from bath towels to DVDs. Within each product category there may be subset categories that also need analysis. These strategies must be considered for all retail stores, taking geographic differences into account as well as determining the content for a retail business's print catalog and/or its virtual Internet business.

Throughout the year, the planner will study the marketplace and the competition to make course corrections for the existing selling year and then modify those projections for the next sales cycle (some sales cycles, such as for clothing, change seasonally, not annually).

Once the plan is made, it then needs to be implemented in retail outlets around the state, nation, or world. Planners work with an array of computerized tools to help determine sales trends as well as the steady supply of inventory. Sometimes there are delays, known as back orders, and they need to be addressed quickly, otherwise customers will leave the store in frustration and possibly never return.

Planners do not work in a vacuum since they often do the actual buying and are in touch with managers who

These merchandise planners put last-minute touches on a wall of art-work hanging in the newest Bloomingdale's department store in New York City. The merchandise arrangement is designed to lure younger shoppers to the chain's downtown location.

oversee stock replenishment. Still, the planner makes a point to maximize every square inch of a store in order to excite customers and increase sales.

Quite often, planners from large retail stores such as Wal-Mart or Sears rely on a tool known as a planogram, which is a schematic drawing of the store. From there, the planner will allocate a large amount of shelf space for one item and possibly less for another. Planograms act as the blueprints for the store managers to follow when instructing employees how to stock the shelves. The planner determines the most logical approach for placing related items together. Socks are placed near undergarments, for example. The planner also needs to consider who the suppliers are and with whom the company has exclusive or specific deals since some manufacturers receive preferential treatment over their competitors, which often means they receive more shelf space. It's all a giant puzzle for the planner and one that needs to be rebuilt throughout the year, or in the case of supermarkets, almost weekly. Some planners will allow for regional differences, too, allowing store managers to make some product placement choices on their own since they know the local shoppers best.

"The planograms—or modulars—make sense insofar as everything fits in the space allotted. Each set is actually constructed at the home office before it reaches the stores. And the layout pages have always explicitly stated that they are 'only a guide' and can be adjusted according to a given store's clientele and needs," notes John Wells, a department manager in one of Wal-Mart's Iowa locations. "The store planners do tour a certain amount of stores in a given year, but the sheer number of Wal-Marts means they'll only visit a fraction of them. The buyers are available by phone and e-mail."

The planner usually works as part of a team with assistants who may be responsible for individual product categories such as notions in a crafts store or socks in a clothing store. The Dollar General chain, for example, has a team of five planners for its nearly 7,000 stores in the United States.

The Bed Bath & Beyond chain requires planners to possess "business knowledge of retail and merchandising concepts and strong problem-solving and analytical skills. Knowledge of planning and allocation systems [is also encouraged]," according to an ad placed on Monster.com.

Education and Training

To perform this job well, most candidates should have some prior retail experience, especially in store planning, inventory management, financial planning, or financial analysis. Retail management or sales skills do not seamlessly allow people to enter this field. Many of the larger chains, such as Federated, offer employees training programs, helping them develop the analytic skills to enhance their abilities.

Lillian Vernon, founder and CEO of the Lillian Vernon Corporation, stands with an assortment of merchandise available through her mail-order catalog at her office in Mount Vernon, New York. Whether a retail operation is a brick-and-mortar store, a Web site, or a print catalog, all of its merchandise together expresses its overall retail presence.

Salary

Planners usually start as hourly employees and are promoted into salaried positions as they advance in seniority.
Geographic variance makes it difficult to determine average
salaries, however. Upscale retail chains will pay between
$65,000 and $100,000 for experienced planners.

Outlook

Jobs in merchandise planning have a strong future over the
next decade. A wise choice for most people looking for a job
with a solid company is to examine its progress over a given
period. Obviously it's more desirable to work as a planner
for a store that has a strong future. Do your research. Is it
a Fortune 500 company? Does it have a strong market
share and a positive image? Bed Bath & Beyond is just one
example of a company that expects a good deal of growth
over the next few years. It has a reputable track record for
meeting and exceeding sales over the past five years and it
opened eighty new stores across the country in 2005.

FOR MORE INFORMATION

ORGANIZATIONS

Center for Retailing Studies

Texas A&M University
Department of Marketing
201 Wehner Building
4112 TAMU
College Station, TX 77843-4112
(979) 845-0325

Institute of Store Planners

25 North Broadway
Tarrytown, NY 10591
(800) 379-9912
Web site: http://www.ispo.org

National Retail Federation

Liberty Place
325 7th Street NW, Suite 1100
Washington, DC 20004
(202) 783-0370
Web site: http://www.nrf.com

WEB SITES

Center for Retailing Studies—Merchandise Planner

http://www.crstamu.org/career_resources/careers-in-
retailing.asp?id=7
This Web site offers a detailed examination of careers in store
planning.

Chain Store Age, an Electronic Industry Journal and Database
http://chainstoreage.com
> This is the electronic component to the trade magazine for store planning professionals

Jobs in Merchandise Planning
http://www.merchandise.planner.jobs.com
> This Web site offers a job board for those people seeking jobs as store planners.

Retail Choice
http://www.retailchoice.com
> This Web site is a job board that lists a variety of national retail job listings.

BOOKS

Institute of Store Planners. *Stores Retail Spaces Six*. Cincinnati, OH: St. Media Group International, 2005.

Israel, Lawrence J. *Store Planning/Design: History, Theory, Process*. Hoboken, NJ: John Wiley & Sons, 1994.

Lopez, Michael J. *Retail Store Planning & Design Manual*. Hoboken, NJ: John Wiley & Sons, 1995.

Varley, Rosemary, and David Gillooley. *Retail Product Management: Buying and Merchandising*. Oxford, England: Routledge Press, 2001.

11

TRAVEL COORDINATOR

A travel coordinator's main job is making a plan to get a person, family, or group from place to place safely and with minimal fuss. Making the trip an enjoyable experience is also a huge factor. The travel coordinator or travel agent is the person people turn to for their travel needs. Travel coordinators and agents either work from home, for an agency, or for a major firm.

Travel consultant Kim Sherwan speaks with a client while seated at her desk at First-Maine Travel Agency in Des Plaines, Illinois. Whether a travel agent works out of his or her home or at a firm, much of his or her time is spent on the telephone making reservations.

Description

More and more, companies that require employees to travel as part of their daily operation hire an in-house staff to effectively control pricing and services. As a result, corporate travel coordinators are a small but growing field. Traditional travel agents have struggled over the past few years given the rise of Internet travel sites and competitive pricing services such as Expedia.com, Priceline.com, and Travelocity.com. Filling the gaps is the independent travel coordinator, someone working independently either in a small office or out of his or her home.

The Minnesota Department of Labor notes, "Airlines no longer pay commissions to travel agencies, which has reduced revenues and caused some agencies to go out of business. However, many consumers still prefer to use a professional travel agent to ensure reliability, to save time, and, in some cases, to save money."

Working as a travel coordinator/agent calls for a diverse set of skills, mainly depending upon the exact job being performed. Since travel arrangements by coordinators or agents are now made electronically, good computer skills top the list of qualifications.

Education and Training

Those who wish to become travel agents should also be excellent communicators since you will be writing or speaking with customers each day. If you run your own service, good math and business skills are also necessary. If you already take classes in a foreign language, you'll be even more qualified when the time comes. Obviously, you also need to have a good handle on world geography.

There are two primary computer software programs—Sabre and Apollo—used by agents to make hotel, plane, and other travel arrangements. These programs are usually taught at training programs that you may be required to take before beginning work in this field. Vocational schools and

Some travel agents handle a variety of specific client requests, including providing traveler's checks, exchanging money, filing for passports, outlining an itinerary in the form of a portfolio, and providing maps and guidebooks.

private firms also offer these courses.

Once at work, agents and coordinators tend to sit at desks or behind counters and field telephone calls or walk-in customers looking for vacation options. Quite often customers have only a vague idea of when and where they want to go and the amount of money they can spend to accomplish the trip. The agent will then explore the options and help shape customers' goals. There are others, however, especially business travelers, who might have exact specifications such as where they need to be and when. In this case, the agent has to match those specifications with the best possible deal. With competing airlines, hotels, package tours, and more, the agent needs to help the customer sift through his or her options. Agents will also be called upon to help travelers solve problems once the trip has begun, which may include a plane breaking down and stranding the customer in the wrong city. As a result, patience is one of the most important job skills a travel agent needs.

For those who prefer to work independently, the personal touch will bring in new business and return customers. For example, an agent sometimes works from his or her home and drums up business by coming up with incentive trips companies can offer employees as rewards or bonuses.

Philip Dunphy
Director of Global Travel Services

Philip Dunphy figures he's one of maybe 1,000 people in the United States who acts as a travel agent for a major corporation. At Pfizer, one of America's leading pharmaceutical firms, Dunphy is a director of global travel services, seeing to it that the company gets its people to and from locations around the world safely and economically. With his staff, Dunphy is on the phone constantly looking for the best deals and arrangements

(continued on page 116)

for a chemist going to a new lab in a foreign city or a research analyst who is bringing a hundred corporate executives from all points of the globe to a single place for a meeting.

Dunphy notes that people can get into this field without a college degree, usually training under someone who is an experienced and certified agent. They need to know Computer Reservation Systems, either the Apollo or Sabre programs, and be very comfortable with computers and the Internet. "Excellent verbal communication skills to effectively handle phone requests" is a must, Dunphy insists. Customer service and knowledge of geography are always seen as pluses on job applications.

"The ability to work in a fast-paced environment and handle multiple requests simultaneously is essential," Dunphy explains. "If you have the ability to defuse upset travelers and resolve problems expeditiously, you're on your way."

Salary

The Department of Labor reports that nationally, the median wage for travel agents is $2,220 per month ($12.80 per hour). Half of all travel agents earn between $1,730 and

$2,800 per month ($10.00 and $16.14 per hour). Certainly these figures could increase if an agent or coordinator works independently from an agency.

Outlook

According to the Minnesota Department of Labor, "The travel industry is sensitive to economic downturns because fewer people go on vacation during these periods. Therefore, the number of job opportunities for travel agents varies with the state of the economy." And the United States Department of Labor sees a 13.2 percent reduction in traditional travel agents through 2012. Currently, there are about 118,000 travel agents with 85 percent of these employees working for travel agencies.

FOR MORE INFORMATION

ORGANIZATIONS

Alliance of Canadian Travel Associations
130 Albert Street, Suite 1705
Ottawa, ON K1P 5G4
Canada
(613) 237-3657
Web site: http://www.acta.ca

American Society of Travel Agents
1101 King Street, Suite 200
Alexandria, VA 22314

(703) 739-2782
Web site: http://www.astanet.com

International Air Transportation Association
800 Place Victoria, P.O. Box 113
Montreal, QC H4Z 1M1
Canada
(514) 390-6840
Web site: http://www.iata.org/atdi

National Association of Commissioned Travel Agents (NACTA)
P.O. Box 2348
Valley Center, CA 92082
(760) 751-1197
Web site: http://www.nacta.com/

The Travel Institute
148 Linden Street
Wellesley, MA 02482
(800) 542-4282
Web site: http://www.thetravelinstitute.com

EDUCATION AND TRAINING

American Society of Travel Agents (ASTA) Educational Programs and Seminars
1101 King Street, Suite 200
Alexandria, VA 22314
(703) 739-2782
Web site: http://www.astanet.com

Travel Agent University
Web site: http://tauniv.com

Travel Education Center (TEC)
Web site: http://www.traveleducation.com/Welcome.html

WEB SITES

American Society of Travel Agents (ASTA) Job Board
Web site: http://www.astanet.com/education/job.asp
  This Web site lists a variety of jobs related to the travel and hospitality industry.

Home-Based Travel Agent
Web site: http://www.Home-Based-Travel-Agent.com
  This Web site provides information about those travel agents who work out of their homes

BOOKS

Eberts, Marjorie, Linda Brothers, and Ann Gisler. *Careers in Travel, Tourism, and Hospitality*. Lincolnwood, IL: VGM Career Horizons, 1997.

Krannich, Ronald, and Caryl Rae Krannich. *Jobs for People Who Love to Travel: Opportunities at Home and Abroad*. 3rd ed. Manassas Park, VA: Impact Publications, 1999.

Monaghan, Kelly. *Home-Based Travel Agent: How to Cash in on the Exciting New World of Travel Marketing*. Branford, CT: Intrepid Traveler, 1999.

Scanlon, Sally. *The Travel Agent's Complete Desk Reference*. Branford, CT: Intrepid Traveler, 2001.

Todd, Ginger, and Susan Rice. *Travel Perspectives: A Guide to Becoming a Travel Agent*. New York, NY: Delmar Publishers, 1995.

PERIODICALS

Travel Agent
One Park Avenue
New York, NY 10016
(212) 951-6600
  This magazine provides a wealth of resources for experienced and beginning travel agents.

12

AUCTIONEER

These days, many people think of auctions as something done entirely on the Internet, but they can be traced back to the early days of bartering and have since spread around the world. People have been auctioning goods for centuries, and the job of auctioneer remains a thriving career opportunity, even today.

Description

The auctioneer does more than most people consider. Besides speaking very fast and forcing the price of an item higher, he or she is a well-informed researcher who knows what an item is worth and the history of its market value. Some auctioneers sell antiques, others sell art, and still others sell agricultural equipment or used cars.

The auctioneer prepares for many hours before the day of the event. He or she is responsible for the appraisal of goods, assembling them, and then advertising the auction. In many cases, such as when entire estates are sold at auction, the auctioneer works closely with the family, company, or agency to maximize the value of the estate's contents.

The National Auctioneers Association states, "The single most important role an auctioneer takes on is that of marketing expert. Auctioneers are adept at marketing a client's property through the appropriate media and reaching a specific audience. In large part, their livelihood depends upon being able to attract those individuals most interested, and therefore, most willing to buy a particular item. The ability to market auctions and merchandise effectively comes from an intimate knowledge of the specific types of merchandise, its value, the demand for such merchandise, and the targeted market.

Auctioneer Darrell Cannon of Palo, Iowa, holds two ceramic vases during an auction in Cedar Rapids, Iowa. Cannon is a 2004 statewide auctioneering champion who makes his living selling items for private estates, organizations, and nonprofits.

"Beyond being able to juggle a number of duties, the prospective auctioneer needs to be personable and work well with a variety of people. During the course of organizing a sale, the auctioneer consults with the seller, fields questions from potential buyers and, on occasion, mediates disputes."

When an auctioneer is hired to handle a sale, his or her first task is to review the items and prepare an evaluation for the seller. The items for sale begin with a "reserved" price, meaning the minimum price for bidding to start. In some cases, it is decided there should be no minimum and then bidding begins with an "absolute" price. This step is the most time-consuming and requires a level of expertise in a number of areas. Some auctioneers specialize in livestock, wine, or fine art, for example. Some auction houses are famous, too, such as Christie's and Sotheby's and have become noteworthy for their high-end art, collectibles, and precious gems.

While reviewing the items, the auctioneer notes the history, background, and condition of the item, information to not only determine the reserved price, but which will also be used during the auction itself.

Once the evaluation is done, the timing and venue for the event must be determined. Not every auction is done at an auction house. Some are done on farm sites, at rodeos, in concert or sports stadiums, or anywhere a large crowd can gather comfortably. Some states even auction off vehicles that have been repossessed, which require a huge amount of space for display and handling.

After the venue is selected, an auction can be advertised. This can start with ads in newspapers or flyers, or it can go all the way up to pricey catalogues. Here, the order of items is determined and the auctioneer carefully sets the pacing of the auction so the most valuable or most unique items go on the block later, keeping people on hand to view the entire auction. It is also important for the auctioneer to maintain control over the auction's tempo and organization in order to maximize sales.

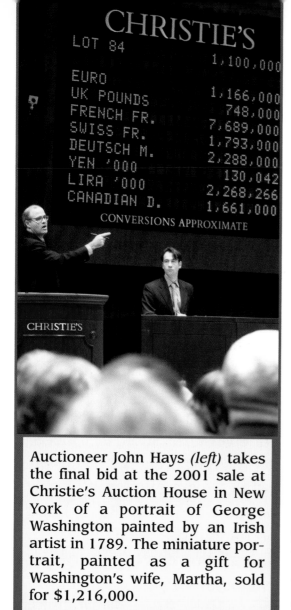

CHRISTIE'S
LOT 84   1,100,000
EURO
UK POUNDS   1,166,000
FRENCH FR.   748,000
SWISS FR.   7,689,000
DEUTSCH M.   1,793,000
YEN '000   2,288,000
LIRA '000   130,042
CANADIAN D.   2,268,266
                    1,661,000
CONVERSIONS APPROXIMATE

CHRISTIE'S

Auctioneer John Hays *(left)* takes the final bid at the 2001 sale at Christie's Auction House in New York of a portrait of George Washington painted by an Irish artist in 1789. The miniature portrait, painted as a gift for Washington's wife, Martha, sold for $1,216,000.

On the day of the auction, the auctioneer welcomes people to the event, allows potential buyers to take a closer look at the items for sale, and surveys the attitude of the crowd. He or she must be careful to control the flow of the event, adjusting the speed as required. As a result, one of the best qualities an auctioneer can have is a quick-thinking mind to anticipate what changes are necessary before they are needed. The audience must be kept interested and entertained by the patter of information at all times.

Other skills recommended for would-be auctioneers include having a strong, clear voice, and a friendly, confident manner. Auctioneers must be able to work with customers and tactfully advise them on an item's value. They must have a wide knowledge of the types of goods that are being auctioned, as well as a good visual memory and a strong business sense in order to understand the legal aspects of the work in detail.

Education and Training

To learn how to be an auctioneer, it helps to gain experience on a volunteer basis at your high school or church. There are many family-run auction businesses and they usually accept entry-level people, starting them in the office and having them learn by assisting current auctioneers. Most auctioneers start out on a part-time basis, learning their craft and their specialties.

There are also numerous schools that teach the business and issue certificates through the National Auctioneers Association. Different states have different licensing requirements, which should be checked when seeking employment. At least 27 states require certification, while all 50 require real estate auctioneers to be licensed. Also, most auctioneers follow the National Auctioneers Association's rules of conduct that enable an auctioneer to earn the trust of a seller. The NAA's Web site adds, "Often licensing boards will waive the educational credits if an applicant served as an apprentice under a licensed auctioneer. Required apprenticeships can range in length from conducting a few auctions under an auctioneer's guidance to one or more years."

The Florida Auctioneer Academy's Web site notes, "Public speaking, leadership background and marketing experience

Terms Heard at Auctions

absentee bid A procedure that allows a person, called an absentee bidder, to participate in the bidding process without being physically present.

agent A person who acts for, or in the place of, another individual or entity by authority from the individual or entity.

appraisal The act or process of estimating value.

auction block The podium or platform where the auctioneer stands while conducting the auction.

bid A prospective buyer's offer of a price he or she will pay to purchase property at auction. Bids are usually in standardized increments established by the auctioneer.

caveat emptor A Latin phrase meaning "let the buyer beware." A legal maxim stating that the buyer takes the risk regarding quality or condition of the property purchased.

due diligence The process of gathering information about the condition and legal status of assets to be sold.

hammer price Price established by the last bidder

and acknowledged by the auctioneer before dropping the hammer or gavel.

opening bid The first bid offered by a bidder at an auction.

sealed bid A method of sale utilized where confidential bids are submitted and later opened at a predetermined place and time.

are useful in developing presentation skills. Technology is rapidly moving into the industry, with computerized clerking and fax marketing, as well as online marketing."

Salary

While most auctioneers work on their own, larger auctions will use assistants called ringmen, either to display items to an audience or to write down bids from the crowd and bring them to the auctioneer. Salaries can vary, but most auctioneers make their money through commissions.

As the sale ends, the auctioneer sees to it that the items are delivered to the proper buyer and that the agreed-upon price has been paid. In some cases this may mean arranging shipping, transport, or careful wrapping for items that were auctioned that day.

For these services, most auctioneers receive an increase in commission, usually a percentage of the total sale that was previously agreed upon. According to the U.S. Department of Labor, the starting salary for auctioneers can be $20,000 with most earning between $50,000 to $100,000 annually.

Outlook

More than two dozen schools teach the skills required for a career in auctioneering. Most every state has a professional organization to oversee auctioneers in their area. While no statistics on career growth are available, America's current interest in auctions is high, fueled by the success of the Web site eBay. Auctioning is likely to be a robust career option in the years ahead.

FOR MORE INFORMATION

ORGANIZATIONS

Auctioneers Association of Canada
10440 156th Street, Suite 305
Edmonton, AB T5P 2R5
Canada
(866) 640-9915
Web site: http://www.auctioneerscanada.com

Bonhams & Butterfields
220 San Bruno Avenue

San Francisco, CA 94103
(415) 861-7500
Web site: http://www.bonhams.com

Heffel—Canada's National Fine Art Auction House
2247 Granville Street
Vancouver, BC V6H 3G1
Canada
(800) 528-9608
Web site: http://www.heffel.com

National Auctioneers Association
8880 Ballentine
Overland Park, KS 66214
(913) 541-8084
Web site: http://www.auctioneers.org

Sotheby's Auction House
1334 York Avenue
New York, NY 10021
(541) 312-6582
Web site: http://www.sothebys.com

WEB SITES
Auction Guide
http://www.auctionguide.com
> The Internet guide to auctions and auctioneers worldwide.

My Little Salesman
http://www.mlsinc.com/home.asp
> This Web site has information about agricultural auctions.

Virtual Inventory Hostin Network
http://www.vihn.net/home.asp
> This Web site is dedicated to solutions for professional auctioneers.

BOOKS

Hildesley, C. Hugh. *The Complete Guide to Buying and Selling at Auction*. New York, NY: W.W. Norton, 1997.

Hindman, Leslie. *Adventures at the Auction: The Ultimate Guide to Buying and Selling at Auction—In Person and Online*. New York, NY: Clarkson Potter, 2001.

Krishna, Vijay. *Auction Theory*. New York, NY: Academic Press, 2002.

Smith, Charles W. *Auctions: The Social Construction of Value*. Berkeley, CA: University of California Press, 1990.

PERIODICALS

Art & Auction
11 E. 36th Street, Ninth Floor
New York, NY 10016
(212) 447-9555
Web site: http://www.artandauction.com
This consumer magazine focuses on high-end auctions, such as those that take place at both Christie's and Sotheby's.

13

IMPORT/ EXPORT SPECIALIST

Goods manufactured overseas have to be imported to the United States for sale, just as goods manufactured here get exported to countries around the globe. Overseeing those transactions, from cars to sneakers, are specialists in shipping.

Description

"Importing is not just for those lone footloose adventurer types who survive by their wits and the skin of their teeth," *Entrepreneur* magazine said in 2001. "It's big business these days—to the tune of an annual $1.2 trillion in goods, according to the U.S. Department of Commerce. Exporting is just as big. In one year alone, American companies exported $772 billion in merchandise to more than 150 foreign countries."

According to the U.S. Census Bureau, the top ten countries with which the United States trades are Canada, Mexico, Japan, China, Germany, the United Kingdom, France, Republic of Korea (South Korea), Taiwan, and Singapore.

What sorts of things are imported or exported? Exports and imports may include raw materials, agricultural products, or manufactured goods, as well as services such as travel, banking, or telecommunications. All goods need to be carefully handled heading into or out of the United States.

Export managers direct foreign sales, negotiate sales and distribution contracts, and arrange payment between manufacturer and retail sales outlet.

Custom brokers are the intermediaries between import/export specialists and customs agents in each country. They prepare the entry papers, file documents to allow delivery of goods, assess duties and taxes that may be charged by any given country, and must be licensed by the United States Department of the Treasury. "For every shipment entering the United States," according to the American

These longshoremen are taking inventory of imported goods in containers that were shipped by boat from foreign countries. Importing and exporting goods is subject to strict and specific restrictions for the health, well-being, and security of U.S. citizens.

Association of Exporters and Importers (AAEI), "there are 500 pages of Customs regulations and thousands of tariff items. The broker must be well versed in determining proper classifications and dutiable value and be fully aware of the vast number of commodities subject to quotas. Customs brokers facilitate release of imported goods, pay required duties, and provide and maintain required records and documents. They may also help clients choose modes of transportation and specific carriers."

Freight forwarders are the agents, licensed by the Federal Maritime Commission or the International Air Transportation Association, for exporters to move cargo overseas. These people need to be familiar with import rules and regulations for each country, have a good working knowledge of United States export regulations, and be familiar with all methods of shipping appropriate to the goods, as well as special packaging needs or handling restrictions. The AAEI says, "Forwarders must be aware of regulations that affect cargo movements, such as hazardous materials rules, special handling or packing restrictions, licensing provisions, and foreign documentation requirements. Forwarders may coordinate arrangements for storage, full-container shipments and inland transportation."

Education and Training

There are several areas of expertise required in the field of exporting with different job functions that slightly overlap. In all cases, training is available either through the employee or specialized schools that can help get you the required licensing. Attributes required for these positions are clear communication skills, good writing skills, and a familiarity with a second or third language.

Salary

A broker is usually paid according to what his or her trade is worth, beginning in the $19,000 to $24,000 range according

In this photograph, a Japanese customs official inspects quarantined oranges imported from the United States. All food items are inspected carefully as they are shipped from country to country. Import and export specialists must pass certification tests in order to ensure that they comply with the strict—and often changing—shipping guidelines between nations.

to the United States Department of Labor. Experienced brokers can earn between $35,000 to $45,000 annually.

Import/export agents are individual contractors who manage import/export activities and coordinate settlements between buyers and sellers. These agents begin in the $16,000 to $20,000 salary range and also can earn up to $35,000 annually with some experience.

Import/Export Terms

Duties and tariffs Taxes levied by the government on the import, export, or use of goods. They are generally based on the value of the goods, or some other factor, such as weight or quantity (specific duties), or a combination of value and other factors (compound duties). Governments may impose tariffs to protect particular domestic industries from imported goods or to raise revenue.

Harmonized Tariff Code Schedule A system for classifying goods in international trade. More than fifty countries use the codes, which were introduced in 1989. The United States International Trade Commission's Office of Tariff Affairs and Trade Agreements is responsible for publishing the annotated Harmonized Tariff Schedule of the United States.

Trade compliance Abidance of countries by active, binding agreements with their trading partners covering imports and exports of goods and services.

Trade security The safety of international shipments of goods and the ability to keep these shipments free of penetration by terrorists or others with illegal intentions.

Outlook

One thing all the jobs in importing and exporting have in common is that their stability and growth are entirely dependent on changing global economic conditions. Still, as the global economy continues to expand, leaving no country and continent unaffected, people will always be required to know how to move goods and materials from one port to the next.

FOR MORE INFORMATION

ORGANIZATIONS

American Association of Exporters and Importers
1050 17th Street NW
Washington, DC 20036
(202) 857-8009
Web site: http://www.aaei.org

Canadian International Freight Forwarders Association
1243 Islington Avenue, Suite 706
Toronto, ON M8X 1Y9
Canada
(416) 234-5100
Web site: http://www.ciffa.com

The National Customs Brokers & Forwarders Association of America, Inc.
1200 18th Street NW, #901

Washington, DC 20036
(202) 466-0222
Web site: http://www.ncbfaa.org

WEB SITES

The Federal Register (Rules and Regulations of Importing/Exporting)
http://www.gpoaccess.gov/fr
> This is the government Web site that contains official information on the importing and exporting of goods.

BOOKS

Nelson, Carl A. *Import/Export: How to Get Started in International Trade.* New York, NY: McGraw-Hill, 2000.
Zodl, Joseph A. *Export Import.* Cincinnati, OH: Betterway Books, 2002.

GLOSSARY

back order Goods that have been ordered but have yet to be delivered by the supplier.

budget An itemized listing of expenditures for a given period, such as a given project. The budget is then used to measure the success or failure of the completed project.

commodity Something useful that can be turned into a commercial advantage.

grant A monetary gift to an institution or a person in order to subsidize a project or program.

inventory A listing describing the quantity of goods and materials at a specific location.

multitask Performing two or more tasks simultaneously, derived from computers and now frequently applied to people.

PDA A lightweight, hand-held, usually pen-based computer used as a personal organizer containing calendar, scheduling, To-Do lists, and sometimes cell phone technology.

promotion A special event designed to increase the sales of a specific item or group of items using an extraordinary touch such as lower prices or bonus items.

purchase order A form that contains pricing, quantity and other purchasing information; most business require purchase orders to confirm that the buying company is committing funds.

seminar A small group engaged in a focused setting, usually under the guidance of a specialist, to thoroughly discuss a topic.

vendor One who sells specific goods or commodities.

workshop An educational series of meetings emphasizing interaction and exchange of information.

INDEX

A

American Association of Exporters and
    Importers (AAEI), 132–133, 134
Americans with Disabilities Act, 67–69
Apollo, 113, 116
auctioneer
    education/training for, 125–127
    job description, 121–125
    resources for, 128–130
    salary of, 127–128

C

Certified Fund Raising Executive
    International, 26
conference planner/conference and meeting
    planner, 63, 65

conference services officer, 63–64
convention coordinator, 64
custom brokers, 132, 133

E
event coordinator
education/training for, 55–58
job description, 53–55
resources for, 61–62
salary of, 59–60
versus wedding/party planner, 52
event planner, 64

F
freight forwarders, 134
fund-raiser
education/training for, 26
job description, 21–25
resources for, 29–30
salary of, 26–28

I
import/export specialist
education/training for, 134
job description, 131–134
resources for, 137–138
salary of, 134–135
import/export terms, 136

L
life coach
education/training for, 90–91
job description, 87–90
resources for, 92–93
salary of, 91

M
meeting planner, 64
Meeting Professionals International, 58, 59
merchandise planner/ assistant planner
education/training for, 107
job description, 103–107
job outlook, 108
resources for, 109–110
salary of, 108

N
National Association of Professional Organizers (NAPO), 78, 79, 80, 82
National Auctioneers Association, 121, 125

O
operations manager
education/training for, 97
job description, 95–97
resources for, 99–101
salary of, 97–98

P
personal assistant
education/training for, 16
job description, 10–15
resources for, 18–19
salary of, 16–17
planogram, 104–105
professional organizer
education/training for, 78–80
job description, 77–78

job outlook, 82
resources for, 83–85
salary of, 80–82

R
retail manager
    education/training for, 35–38
    job description, 32–35
    resources for, 39–41
    salary of, 38

S
Sabre, 113, 116

T
trade-show organizer
    education/training for, 69–70
    job description, 64–69

resources for, 73–75
responsibilities of, 65–66
salary of, 70
travel coordinator
    education/training for,
        113–115
    job description, 112–113
    resources for, 117–119
    salary of, 116

W
wedding/party planner
    education/training for,
        44–49
    job description, 43–44
    resources for, 50–51
    salary of, 49

About the Author

Robert Greenberger has been organizing things all his life, starting with a series of jobs at his high school and college newspapers. At DC Comics, he was manager of editorial operations, and at Marvel Comics, he was director of publishing operations. A graduate of SUNY-Binghamton, he is currently a senior editor at DC Comics and a writer, which requires a careful balance between professional and home obligations. He makes his home in Connecticut with his wife, Deb, and children, Kate and Robbie.

Photo Credits

Cover © www.istockphoto.com/Lise Gagne; pp. 9, 11 © age fotostock/SuperStock; p. 14 © Warner Bros. Television/Getty images; 17 © Max Franklin/Getty images; pp. 31, 32, 112 © Tim Boyle/Getty images; p. 104 © Chris Hondros/Getty images; pp. 20, 25 © AP/Wide World Photos/Joe Rowley; p. 22 © AP/ Wide World Photos/Clement Britt; p. 34 © Omni Photo Communications Inc./Index Stock Imagery; pp. 42, 46, 63, 64, 124 © Reuters/ Corbis; p.44 © AP/ Wide World Photos/Paul Middlestaedt; pp. 52, 53 © Jon Feingersh/Corbis; p. 56 www. fiurproductions.com; p. 59 © AP/ Wide World Photos/Peter Cosgrove; pp. 68, 72 © AP/ Wide World Photos/Reed Saxon; pp. 76, 77 © Philip James Corwin/Corbis; p. 79 © Maria Hesse/ Imagestate; pp. 86, 88 © AP/Wide World Photos/Kimm Anderson; p. 90 © Eric Kamp/ Index Stock Imagery; pp. 94, 96 © AP/Wide World Photos/Mike Valeri; p. 98 © AP/Wide World Photos/ Douglas Healey; pp. 102, 106 © AP/Wide World Photos/Richard Harbus; pp. 111, 114 © Bob Wickley/SuperStock; pp. 120, 122 © AP/Wide World Photos/ Charlie Neibergall; pp. 131, 133 © Gabe Palmer/Corbis; p. 135 © Tom Wagner.

Designer: Evelyn Horovicz; Editor: Joann Jovinelly